Withdrawn

P9-DNF-876

Northville District Library
212 W. Cady Street
Northville, MI 48187-15

Also by Phillip Hoose

It's Our World, Too!
Young People Who Are Making a Difference
How They Do It—How You Can, Too!

We Were There, Too!
Young People in U.S. History

Hey, Little Ant
(with Hannah Hoose)

THE RACE TO SAVE THE LORD GOD BIRD

THE RACE TO SAVE THE LORD GOD BIRD

PHILLIP HOOSE

MELANIE KROUPA BOOKS
FARRAR, STRAUS AND GIROUX • NEW YORK

Front jacket illustrations: *Ivory-billed Woodpecker* (detail) from *The Birds of America* by John James Audubon (New York: J. J. Audubon; Philadelphia: J. B. Chevalier, 1840–44). National Audubon Society, courtesy of Susan Roney Drennan. Background map: *A Nineteenth-Century View of North America—1865* by G. W. Colton, from *The United States in Old Maps and Prints* by Eduard Van Ermen (Wilmington, Del.: Atomium Books, 1990)

Text copyright © 2004 by Phillip Hoose
Maps copyright © 2004 by Jeffrey L. Ward
All rights reserved
Distributed in Canada by Douglas & McIntyre Ltd.
Printed in China by South China Printing Co. Ltd.
Designed by Barbara Grzeslo
First edition, 2004
10 9 8 7 6 5 4 3 2 1

www.fsgkidsbooks.com

Library of Congress Cataloging-in-Publication Data
Hoose, Phillip M., date.
    The race to save the Lord God Bird / by Phillip Hoose.— 1st ed.
        p. cm.
    Summary: Tells the story of the Ivory-billed Woodpecker's decline in the United States, describing the encounters between this species and humans, and discussing what these encounters have taught us about preserving endangered species and habitat.
        ISBN 0-374-36173-8
        1. Ivory-billed woodpecker—Juvenile literature. 2. Endangered species—Juvenile literature. [1. Ivory-billed woodpecker. 2. Woodpeckers. 3. Endangered species.] I. Title.

    QL696.P56H66   2004
    598.7'2—dc22

                                                                2003049049

Northville District Library
212 West Cady Street
Northville MI 48167

JUN 0 1 2005

3 9082 09819 7059

In memory of James Tanner,
and to the many biologists and conservationists to come
who will continue his work
by preserving species in their habitats

James Tanner

And to Giraldo Alayón,
who, like the Ivory-bill itself,
balances science and magic in Cuba

Giraldo Alayón with
sons Giraldo (*left*)
and Julio, in 1987

CONTENTS

THE RACE TO SAVE THE LORD GOD BIRD

INTRODUCTION
A BIRD OF THE SIXTH WAVE

To become extinct is the greatest tragedy in nature. Extinction means that all the members of an entire species are dead; that an entire genetic family is gone, forever. Or, as ornithologist William Beebe put it, "When the last individual of a race of living things breathes no more, another heaven and another earth must pass before such a one can be again."

Some might argue that this doesn't seem so tragic. After all, according to scientists, 99 percent of all species that have ever lived are now extinct. And there have already been at least five big waves of mass extinction, caused by everything from meteorites to drought. The fifth and most recent wave, which took place a mere 65 million years ago, destroyed the dinosaurs along with about two-thirds of all animal species alive at that time. In other words, we've been through this before.

But the sixth wave, the one that's happening now, is different. For the first time, a single species, *Homo sapiens*—humankind—is wiping out thousands of life forms by consuming and altering the earth's resources. Humans now use up more than half of the world's fresh water and nearly half of everything that's grown on land. The sixth wave isn't new; it started about twelve thousand years ago when humans began clearing land to plant food crops. But our impact upon the earth is accelerating so rapidly now that thousands of species are being lost every year. Each of these species belongs to a complicated web of energy and activity called an ecosystem. Together, these webs connect the smallest mites to the greatest trees.

This is a story about a species of the sixth wave, a species that was—and maybe still is—a bird of the deep forest. It took only a century for *Campephilus principalis*, more commonly known as the Ivory-billed Woodpecker, to slip from a flourishing life in the sunlit forest canopy to a marginal existence in the shadow of extinction. Many species declined during that same century, but the Ivory-bill became the singular object of a tug-of-war between those who destroyed and sold its habitat and a new breed of scientists and conservationists dedicated to preserving species by saving habitat. In some ways, the Ivory-bill was the first modern endangered species, in that some of the techniques used today to try to save imperiled plants and animals were pioneered in the race to rescue this magnificent bird.

I say the Ivory-bill "maybe still is" a bird of the deep forest because some observers, including some very good scientists, believe that a few Ivory-bills continue to exist. Since I first became interested in birds in 1975, I have read or heard dozens of reports that someone has just caught a fresh glimpse or heard the unmistakable call of the Ivory-bill. Again and again, even the slimmest of rumors sends hopeful bird-watchers lunging for their boots, smearing mosquito repellent onto their arms, and bolting out the door to look for it. Year after year they return with soggy boots, bug-bitten arms, and no evidence.

The Ivory-bill is a hard bird to give up on. It was one of the most impressive creatures ever seen in the United States. Those who wrote about it—from John James Audubon to Theodore Roosevelt—were astonished by its beauty and strength. They gave it names like "Lord God bird" and "Good God bird." Fortunately, in 1935, when there were just a few left, four scientists from Cornell University took a journey deep into a vast, primitive swamp and came back with a sound recording of the phantom's voice and twelve seconds of film that showed the great bird in motion. It was a gift from, and for, the ages.

Cornell's image sparked a last-ditch effort led by the Audubon Society to save the Ivory-bill in its wilderness home before it was too late. But others were equally intent on clearing and selling the trees before the conservationists could rescue the species.

The race to save the Ivory-bill became an early round in what is now a worldwide struggle to save endangered species. Humans challenged the Ivory-bill to adapt very quickly to rapidly shifting circumstances, but as events unfolded, the humans who tried to rescue the bird had to change rapidly, too. The Ivory-bill's saga—perhaps unfinished—continues to give us a chance to learn and adapt. As we consider the native plants and animals around us, we can remind ourselves of the race to save the Lord God bird and ask, "What can we do to protect them in their native habitats while they're still here with us?"

PROLOGUE
THE HOSTAGE

A majestic and formidable species . . . his eye is brilliant and daring, and his whole frame
so admirably adapted for his mode of life and method of procuring subsistence, as to
impress on the mind of the examiner the most reverential ideas of the Creator.

—Alexander Wilson, writing about the Ivory-billed Woodpecker

Wilmington, North Carolina — February 1809

ALEXANDER WILSON CLUCKED HIS HORSE SLOWLY ALONG THE MARGIN OF A SWAMP IN North Carolina. Bending forward in the saddle, he squinted out at the small birds that flitted across the moss-bearded boughs of giant cypress trees, hoping he could get a clear shot without going into the water. When he heard the first call of an Ivory-billed Woodpecker, he knew what it was instantly, even though he had never seen one before. Here was the toot of a toy horn everyone had told him to expect, repeated again and again. Then came the two-note *ba-DAM*, a crack of bone against wood that shot through the swamp. When you hear that, everyone had said, then you'll know you're really in the South.

Wilson's heart must have been racing as he dismounted and crept toward the bird, said to be as big as a rooster, with bold black-and-white plumage and an outsized bill that gleamed in the sun like polished ivory. The power of this bird was legendary. A century before, the British explorer Mark Catesby had stood beneath a tree and watched in awe as an Ivory-bill, digging for insects, ripped away huge sheets of bark, sending down a bushel basket's worth of wood in less than an hour. Even President

Thomas Jefferson had written about "the white-bill woodpecker." Here was a meeting Wilson had long anticipated.

He moved slowly, for he was a walking powder keg. Wilson kept a loaded pistol in each pocket, a loaded rifle strapped across his shoulder, a pound of gunpowder in a flask, and five pounds of gunpowder on his belt. This was not only for the Indians, robbers, panthers, and bears he might encounter in his travels. Gunpowder was a tool of his trade, like paint. Wilson was on a mission to paint and describe every single bird species in the new United States of America. Once he was finished, he would compile the portraits and accounts into a set of volumes and sell them. He believed there were enough people who wanted to know about the birds of the new nation to provide him a living. For now, he was asking them to buy subscriptions to his work, to pay him in advance and have faith that he would finish the paintings and mail off the books—in other words, to invest in *him*. Though he was hardly rich, Wilson was off to a good start, having sold subscriptions to President Jefferson and most members of his cabinet.

Wilson preferred to sketch live birds if he could trap them, but usually he couldn't. So he shot them out of trees and shrubs and marshes, firing off a hailstorm of small steel pellets that struck the birds in a deadly mist. He hoped that no single ball would tear their feathers too badly or mangle their features beyond recognition. He also hoped they wouldn't be disfigured when they fell and struck the ground. He collected the carcasses and skinned them, removing their internal organs so they wouldn't rot, then packed them in salt and stuffed them full of cotton until his journey was over and he would have time to paint them.

When Wilson finally got a clear look at the Ivory-bill, he steadied his shotgun, aimed carefully, and killed the bird cleanly. He fetched it from the base of the tree and placed it in his collection bag. Hours later he brought down another Ivory-bill, and was probably still smiling about his good luck when he came upon yet a third peeling bark from the high branches of an enormous cypress tree. The big male's red crest glowed like a flame in the sunlight.

Again Wilson fired, sending another trophy to the ground. When Wilson got to it, this bird was still moving, having been wounded only slightly in one wing. Delighted, Wilson flung his coat over the woodpecker to calm it down and carried it slowly back

ALEXANDER WILSON

"His eyes were piercing, dark and luminous and his nose looked like a beak," wrote Charles Leslie of his hero Alexander Wilson. Leslie started working for Wilson at the age of seventeen, coloring in the sketches of American birds that Wilson had drawn. "I remember the extreme accuracy of his drawings," wrote Leslie, "and how carefully he had counted the number of scales on the tiny legs and feet of his subjects."

Born in Scotland, Wilson became known as the "Father of Ornithology" in the United States after the publication of his nine-volume work American Ornithology. *Wilson spent many years traveling on horseback throughout the eastern United States, collecting specimens and painting birds at a time when many of the continent's birds were unknown. He carefully and sometimes beautifully described the range, habitat, and behavior of our birds. A petrel, a plover, a warbler, and even a whole genus of warblers still bear Wilson's name.*

to his horse. As he planted his foot in the stirrup and swung his leg over the saddle, the bird exploded into life with a shriek resembling "the violent crying of a young child." The horse bolted for the swamp. Wilson seized the reins with one hand and tried to keep hold of the bird with the other, finally calming at least the horse. "It nearly cost me my life," he later wrote.

The bird shrieked all the way into the town of Wilmington, twelve miles down the road. As the strange trio—frazzled naturalist, bulging-eyed horse, and wailing woodpecker—careened through the streets of Wilmington, startled townspeople rushed to their doors and windows, their faces filled with concern.

Reaching a hotel, Wilson tied his horse and took the bird inside. It was still wailing under his coat as the landlord and curious guests clustered around. Wilson asked for a room for himself and "my baby," and then, to satisfy the curious, he lifted the coat from the bird. When the laughter died down, he took the Ivory-bill to his room and left it there, locking the door behind him. Then he went back outside to tend to his horse.

A few minutes later, he turned the key to his door again and pushed it open. The air was thick with dust. Chunks of plaster covered his bed. Anchored to a window frame, near the ceiling, the woodpecker was smashing away at the wall with sideways strokes of its mighty bill. Already it had torn a fifteen-inch-square crater in the wall, and it was just seconds away from piercing through to the outside and making its escape.

As Wilson lunged for it, the bird snapped its beak and slashed back with dagger-sharp claws. Wilson finally managed to loop a string over one leg. Pulling the bird down, Wilson fastened it to a table and went outside again to catch his breath and try to find some food for the woodpecker. Wilson realized the creature must be starving, but he probably had no idea what he could find in Wilmington that an Ivory-billed Woodpecker would eat. This time, when Wilson returned, he opened the door of his hotel room and found the bird perched atop a pile of mahogany chips—the ruins of the hotel's table. The bird puffed up its feathers, swung its head around, and glared at Wilson through a furious yellow eye.

That was enough. Wilson grabbed his sketchboard and began to draw while he still had a room. Whenever he edged too close to the bird, he paid a price in blood. He wrote of the Ivory-bill: "While [I drew him] he cut me severely in several places and, on the whole, displayed such a noble and unconquerable spirit, that I was frequently tempted to restore him to his native woods. He lived with me nearly three days, but refused all sustenance, and I witnessed his death with regret."

Head of the Pileated Woodpecker, size of life.

Head of the Ivory-billed Woodpecker, size of life.

1. Ivory billed Woodpecker reduced.
2. Pileated W. reduced.
3. Red-headed W. drawn by the same scale.

Wilson's Ivory-bill (*upper right and lower middle*) shares the page in his *American Ornithology* with two Pileated Woodpeckers and a Red-headed Woodpecker (*lower right*)

Ivory-billed
Woodpecker
specimens at the
Louisiana State
University Museum
of Natural Science

CHAPTER ONE
SPECIMEN 60803

Nature does nothing uselessly.

—Aristotle

Louisiana State University — February 2002

Dr. James Van Remsen pulls open a wooden drawer and hands me an Ivory-billed Woodpecker. It's dead, of course, one of seven Ivory-bill specimens in a dark room of the Louisiana State University Museum of Natural Science. It feels light and stiff—more like an object than a creature that once lived and breathed. Its wings are folded tightly in on themselves like an umbrella. The hollow eyes have been stuffed with cotton. The backswept crest of this male is more orange than red now, and the bill has darkened from ivory to tarnished gold. Dangling by a string from one gray ankle is a white tag that says "*CAMPEPHILUS PRINCIPALIS*—lsumz 60803; male."

I raise it up against a fluorescent light to inspect it more closely. Somehow the Ivory-bill looks both prehistoric and futuristic at the same time. The faded red crown of this big male shoots stiffly back like the bony crest of a pterodactyl, the ancient winged reptile. By contrast, other specimens show that the female has a jet-black crown that nods slightly forward and ends in a sharp point. In both sexes, a bold white stripe starts below each ear and snakes down the long neck, zagging below the shoulder and then flaring out into a white saddle that blankets the lower wing.

Any species in nature, from the tiniest insect to the Blue Whale, is a collection of design experiments, field-tested and remodeled again and again over thousands of years. By looking carefully at the way a bird is built and then thinking backward—asking questions like "Why would a wing be so long?" or "Why are its eyes on the sides of the head instead of the front?"—it's possible to get some sense of how the bird got its food and defended itself, how widely it traveled, and what role it might have had within its ecosystem.

Of course my attention goes first to the amazing bill. It's not really made of ivory, like an elephant's tusk, but of bone, covered by a sheath of a special protein called keratin. It's broad at the base, and rooted deep into the bird's thick-boned skull to absorb the shock of pounding a tree. Its slitlike nostrils are fringed with hair to keep out sawdust. An Ivory-bill needed this big, stout crowbar of a bill to pry strips of bark off a tree, because its favorite food lay just underneath. The Ivory-bill ate some fruits and berries when they were in season, but mostly it ate grubs—the larvae of beetles. Certain kinds of beetle would attack a dying or injured tree by boring through the bark to lay their eggs, which hatched into stout, wormlike creatures—the grubs. Ivory-bills used their bills to peel the bark away from the tree and get at these fat delicacies—which were then exposed under the bark—like thieves robbing a safe.

As LSU specimen 60803 shows plainly, the bill was far more than just a crowbar. Its tip is a miniature chisel, engineered for the fine work of flicking out and nabbing the startled grubs that tried to squirm away. If they got too far, the Ivory-bill had one more tool to finish the job—a hard-tipped tongue lined with needle-sharp barbs. The tongue was so long that it wrapped around the inside of the bird's skull and could be zapped out in an instant to spear a fugitive grub.

A woodpecker's bill has to keep growing constantly throughout its life because it keeps getting worn down by smacking against wood. The same is true of a beaver's front teeth. However, there is one amazing Ivory-bill specimen in a Cuban museum whose upper bill kept growing for some rea-

---

WEIGHT-SAVING FEATURES

Specimen 60803 is nearly two feet long, but even when it was alive and still possessed all its internal organs, it weighed barely a pound. Like most birds, Ivory-bills had to be light so they could fly. Their weight-saving features included the following:

- *Thin, hollow bones filled with "struts," allowing air spaces that provide strength without adding weight.*
- *No jawbone, no teeth, and no vertebrae in their tails.*
- *A reproduction system with "external eggs," which relieves the mother of the weight of a young bird developing within her body.*
- *Many neck vertebrae make it possible to reach objects with their bills instead of having to use limbs, which would add weight.*
- *A kite-like skeleton with fewer bones than most mammals have; the bones are fused together, providing support for flight.*

son until it curled over the lower bill and continued on in a great arc all the way under its body. This incredible bill made the bird unable to attack trees, but it could still open its lower bill to take food. Its parents kept it alive for more than a year by feeding it termites.

Famous Cuban Ivory-bill specimen collected by Johannes Gundlach in the mid-nineteenth century

I push back specimen 60803's tag to examine a foot. Four scaly, dagger-sharp toes are clenched into a tight claw. One toe points downward, a second and third point forward, and the fourth sticks out to the side. Being able to spread out its toes helped this bird attach itself to bark and hitch its way up tree trunks and out along tree limbs. Stiff tail feathers braced it against the trunk and kept it from falling backward as it pounded away. And, as Alexander Wilson found out in his hotel room, those sharp toes could turn into deadly weapons. "When taken by the hand," wrote Wilson, "they strike with great violence, and inflict very severe wounds with their bill as well as claws, which are extremely sharp and strong."

As specimen 60803's tag says, the Ivory-bill's scientific name is *Campephilus principalis*, or "principal lover of caterpillars." The Ivory-bill is one of eleven species in the genus *Campephilus*, found mainly in hot, tropical climates. Almost all members of the genus have black-and-white feathering, which helps them blend in with tree bark, and in most species the male has a red crest. All eleven *Campephilus* woodpeckers rap out the same message, a sharp two-note "*ka-BLACK!*" delivered to tell family members where they are or to warn away any creature that might be thinking about invading a feeding or nesting area.

DARWIN'S FINCHES

While exploring the Galápagos Islands far off the coast of South America, British scientist Charles Darwin (1809–1882) encountered a bizarre assortment of plants and animals, including swimming lizards and flightless birds.

Darwin was fascinated by the fourteen species of finch he saw. Each had a different-shaped beak and a different way of getting food with it. One sipped nectar, another cracked seeds, another scraped small insects off leaves.

Darwin came to believe that each finch species had "evolved" from a small group of birds once blown onto the Galápagos by a storm. These ancestors had landed in a kind of paradise, with no natural enemies. They could multiply until they reached the limit of their food supply. Then they had to find a new way to obtain food, or die. Darwin theorized that finches' bills were visible records of at least fourteen such changes, or "adaptations." After many generations, each type had changed so much it could reproduce only with its own kind and became a separate species.

CAMPEPHILUS PRINCIPALIS **(PART I)**

In 1753 Swiss biologist Carl von Linné, known as Linnaeus, developed a system that allowed every species of plant and animal in the world to be identified by its own sequence of Latin names. This enabled people of different languages and regions of the world to talk about the same bird, mammal, reptile, fish, insect, or plant, no matter what they called it locally. This was especially important for a creature like the Ivory-billed Woodpecker, which was called by dozens of nicknames.

For example, specimen 60803 might have been called a "Kent" or a "Lord God bird" in one part of Louisiana, but something entirely different even a county over. Using Linnaeus's system, everyone could know this bird by its genus name, Campephilus, *and its species name,* principalis.

Specimen 60803's wings also offer clues about its life. Its long, tapered wings and streamlined tail feathers propelled it great distances to search for weakened, dying, grub-infested trees. The Ivory-bill helped regenerate the forest by starting the job of breaking apart and toppling dying trees. The trees in old forests where most Ivory-bills lived had wide-spreading limbs whose summer leaves formed a green shield that blocked sunlight from reaching the ground. The forest was dark underneath these trees. In order for sunlight to reach the ground so that new seedlings could germinate, a tree had to fall and open a hole in the canopy. Ivory-bills stripped the still-tight bark from the dying tree as they searched for grubs. Then smaller woodpeckers, ants, grubs, and other creatures could attack the tree in shifts, weakening it further until it finally fell over.

For thousands and thousands of years, Ivory-billed Woodpeckers had a steady, secure existence. They mated for life, roamed the forest in pairs, and could live to be as old as thirty. Females laid only two or three shiny white eggs at a time—the fewest of any North American woodpecker—but they didn't need to lay many, since Ivory-bills were big and powerful enough to defend themselves against almost all predators.

I hold 60803 up close to read the rest of the specimen tag: "ROARING BAYOU, FRANKLIN PARISH; 12 JULY 1899; COLLECTED BY GEORGE E. BEYER." Who was George E. Beyer? Why did he kill and stuff this bird, and how did it end up in the LSU museum? I decide to try to find out. Whoever he was, I suspected that by 1899, when Mr. Beyer met the future specimen 60803, things were changing fast for the Ivory-bill, and not for the better.

THE SHOWMAN

George Beyer began each day by waxing the ends of his handlebar mustache to needle-sharp perfection. His appearance was important. Besides being a first-rate biologist, Professor Beyer had a showman's flair for attracting attention. Once he invited a newspaper reporter to witness as a small rattlesnake bit his pinky finger for several days in a row.

It was his way of testing the new theory of inoculation—the notion that a person could build resistance against an infectious substance by injecting small amounts of the substance itself. The reporter relayed the shocking experiment to papers throughout the United States and Germany. Thousands of readers hotly debated whether Professor Beyer was a visionary or a downright fool. He survived, and went on to give packed public lectures on topics such as poisonous snakes, Indian mounds, and yellow fever.

As a boy in his native Germany, George Beyer had become so skilled at museum work that he was sent, at the age of eighteen, to Central America by himself to collect insects, reptiles, and birds for the Dresden Zoological Museum. After a year's painstaking work, Beyer carefully packed all the labeled specimens into crates and put them aboard a ship bound for Germany. When he learned that everything had been lost in a shipwreck, he couldn't bring himself to go back home. Instead, he bought a steamship ticket to the United States.

Despite his thick German accent, he had no trouble finding work. Taxidermy—preparing specimens—was so important that Beyer's skills were in hot demand. In 1893 he was hired to build a first-class natural history museum at Tulane University in New Orleans. From then on, George Beyer was always on the lookout for a rare or exotic specimen that would boost the museum's reputation and pull in visitors.

When Beyer first heard a report in 1899 that there were still Ivory-billed Wood-

CAMPEPHILUS PRINCIPALIS **(PART II)**

Linnaeus's framework for classifying and naming plants and animals had seven parts. The Ivory-billed Woodpecker, like all animals, is in the kingdom *Animalia (about 1.07 million species named so far). Because it has vertebrae—hollow sections of backbone strung like beads onto a nerve cord—the Ivory-bill belongs to the* phylum *Chordata (about 45,000 named species). So do humans. All of the world's bird species belong to the* class *Aves (9,757 species). All woodpeckers and several other bird families are of the* order *Piciformes (375 species).*

Woodpeckers alone belong to the family *Picidae (179 species), distinguished from other Piciformes mainly by the arrangement of their toes—two facing forward and two back. The family is divided into 33 woodpecker* genera—*plural for* genus. *The Ivory-bill's genus is* Campephilus, *whose 11 species tend to be large black-and-white woodpeckers found in warm regions. Finally, the Ivory-bill specifically is identified by its* species *name,* principalis—*first among all. So while the Ivory-bill could be introduced at fancy occasions as* Animalia Chordata Aves Piciformes Picidae Campephilus principalis, *we save our breath and call it by its genus and species name—*Campephilus principalis.

peckers left in Louisiana, he didn't believe it. His doubt vanished instantly when, as he wrote, "a gentleman handed me the dried head of a female Ivory-bill . . . informing me that he could guide me to the spot where he had shot it and several others."

To bring back the skin of an Ivory-billed Woodpecker! That would fill the museum with visitors and would rank among the crowning achievements of Beyer's scientific career. Beyer waited until Tulane's summer break, hired horses and guides, and then set off in July, at the very height of mosquito season. By mid-month the party had hacked and swatted its way into a wilderness swamp in northeast Louisiana that locals called Big Lake. As soon as they broke through a perimeter of thick brush to the cypress-ringed lake, Beyer knew he had struck gold. "We could hear quite frequently the rather plaintiff [sic] but loud cry of the 'Log-god' for such the bird is called by those acquainted with it in that section of the state," he wrote.

Beyer found and killed seven Ivory-billed Woodpeckers during his weeklong expedition. The highlight of his trip arrived when his eyes came to rest on a large rectangular hole near the top of a dead elm tree. Concealed behind a thick growth of poison ivy was a large, freshly cut hole. It was an Ivory-bill's nest! "There was but one young one about," Beyer noted, "and it remained in close vicinity of the entrance, notwithstanding that it was almost fully feathered and able to fly. Both parents were still feeding it."

Beyer shot the entire family, cut down the top of the tree, and made an exhibit of the nest in the Tulane Museum. The Ivory-bill family attracted visitors like a magnet. As he wrote proudly (but incorrectly) to W. D. Rogers, acting president of Tulane, "it is doubtful whether any other institution outside of the U.S. National Museum possesses more than a single specimen of this species. This one group alone as it now stands in the [Tulane] Museum represents easily a value of $250."

In the 1930s, a few years after George Beyer's death, the stuffed specimens from his Big Lake trip were transferred from Tulane to the LSU museum. Seventy or so years later I hold the adult male of the family, now LSU specimen number 60803, in my hands as Dr. Remsen waits for me to finish with it. I feel transported for a few moments to the great lost forest over which this stiff, faded object once reigned. This bird heard Red Wolves howl and panthers scream. While the drumbeat of rain pelted the shiny green leaves of its poison ivy curtain, it protected its eggs in a cozy hole high above the ground.

Finally it is time for me to put 60803 back into its case. I'm filled with questions as I think about how the Ivory-bill survived so well for many thousands of years. But then, in the ninety years that passed between 1809, when Alexander Wilson shot his Ivory-bills to paint them, and 1899, when George Beyer shot his to exhibit them in a museum, the Ivory-bill's world collapsed. What happened? I'm determined to find out. To start, I have to go back to the early 1800s and meet another great painter of birds.

The Ivory-billed Woodpecker's powerful bill could pry the bark back from even the stoutest limbs

Audubon's original watercolor painting of the Golden Eagle includes this tiny figure of a hunter crossing a chasm on a log. Many believe it is a miniature self-portrait reflecting Audubon's own struggle to track down birds and complete *The Birds of America*

CHAPTER TWO
AUDUBON ON THE IVORY-BILLED FRONTIER

He neglects his material interests and is forever wasting his time hunting, drawing and
stuffing birds, and playing the fiddle. We fear he will never be fit for any
practical purpose on the face of the Earth.

—John James Audubon's brother-in-law

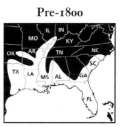

Pre-1800

Southern Rivers and States—1820-1835

On October 12, 1820, thirty-five-year-old John James Audubon pushed his flowing, shoulder-length hair back from his face, kissed his wife, Lucy, and their two young sons goodbye, and climbed aboard a flatboat bound for New Orleans from Cincinnati. His worldly possessions included his gun, his drawing supplies, a roll of wire, a few books, a brass telescope, and the buckskin clothes on his back. His lone companion was thirteen-year-old Joseph Mason, a boy with a genius for painting flowering plants and trees, perfect for the backgrounds Audubon would need to complete his great project.

Audubon didn't even have enough money to book passage. He signed on as a hunter whose job would be to shoot game to feed the crew and passengers. But as they pushed off down the Ohio River, Audubon must have felt like a rich man, for he was finally following his dream. He was fed up with teaching dancing and giving drawing instructions to students with modest talents; he was tired of being a shopkeeper. Now he was determined to do what he cared about most: paint birds. Not just a few species, either, but all the birds of America.

As a free-spirited boy in the French countryside, Audubon had filled his room

The white area shows the wide expanse of the Ivory-bill's original distribution. The bird might have been found within this area—although only in places where the habitat was suitable—but not outside it

John James Audubon, engraving by John Sartain, based on a painting by F. Cruikshanks

with nests and birds' eggs and animal skins, which he practiced drawing over and over. His father sent him to America in 1803 to take care of property he had recently bought there, and to avoid having his son serve in Napoleon's army. Arriving in Pennsylvania at the age of eighteen, Audubon was only about ten years younger than the United States of America itself.

France was settled, but America seemed new, vast, and barely explored. After Audubon married Lucy Bakewell, in 1808, the couple opened a store with a third partner in the Ohio River town of Louisville, Kentucky, selling goods to settlers and frontier families. But life behind a counter didn't suit Audubon. He loved to roam the woods, sleeping on the ground in Indian camps. He scrapped his frilly white shirts and black satin breeches for shirts and leggings fashioned of deerskin. His leather belt held a sheath knife and a tomahawk. He sometimes slicked his long hair with bear grease. He played his fiddle and danced, and charmed nearly everyone he met. But despite his optimistic nature, he couldn't seem to figure out a way to earn a living that would make him happy.

Audubon's life changed one day in March 1810 when Alexander Wilson, the renowned bird artist, turned up at the store. Wilson proudly untied a folio of his bird paintings, laying them out for Audubon to see. To Wilson's astonishment, Audubon pulled out bird paintings of his own, and as they compared the two sets of images, both men may have instantly recognized that Audubon's were better. Wilson's birds looked stiff, because they had been painted mainly from stuffed specimens. Already

Audubon was developing an entirely different style. He had signed even his first sketches "Drawn *from nature* by J. J. Audubon." The encounter with Wilson planted the seed that would form Audubon's own future: he, too, would paint the birds of the new country, but he would paint *his* in natural poses, using all the extravagant colors of their feathering, showing them doing the things birds actually did, like fashioning nests and tearing at prey. He would paint them in natural settings so that he could reveal not only how the birds behaved but what America looked like.

So it was that ten years later, in the fall of 1820, after a disastrous few years in which he lost his business, had to declare bankruptcy, and even spent a few weeks in prison, Audubon decided he could wait no longer. Like Wilson, he would paint the birds of America and publish the art in a collection of volumes. Lucy supported this plan and agreed to raise their sons alone during his absence. Together with his young apprentice, Mason, Audubon spent sixteen months searching the wilderness for birds and traveling the Ohio and Mississippi rivers. Audubon and Mason often jumped off the boat and went out to shoot birds in the swamps and forests and marshes along the slow-moving Ohio, collecting the specimens that Audubon would later paint. Often they slept wrapped in buffalo robes and went long periods without eating.

As they floated down the Ohio, they heard a few Ivory-billed Woodpeckers calling from the adjacent trees, but once the Ohio joined the Mississippi River at Cairo, Illinois, forming a mighty current that swept them south toward the Gulf of Mexico at four miles an hour, the Ivory-bill's *pait pait pait*, as Audubon described it, was almost constantly audible from the distant forests on either side.

On December 20, 1820, they gunned down an Ivory-bill in a swamp forest near the junction of the Arkansas and Mississippi rivers. Though its wing was broken, it tried to survive, playing dead at the base of a tree until the approaching footsteps drew too near. Then "it Jumped up and climbed a tree fast as a squirel to the very top . . .

"WOULD THAT I COULD"

Few who read Audubon's forbidding description of Ivory-bill country made quick plans to visit. He wrote:

> *I wish, kind reader, it were in my power to present to your mind's eye the favorite resort of the Ivory-billed woodpecker. Would that I could describe the extent of those deep morasses, spreading their sturdy moss-covered branches, as if to admonish intruding man to pause and reflect on the many difficulties which he must encounter . . .*
>
> *Here and there, as [the adventurer] approaches an opening that proves merely a lake of black muddy water, his ear is assailed by the dismal croaking of innumerable frogs, the hissing of serpents, or the bellowing of alligators!*
>
> *Would that I could give you an idea of the sultry pestiferous atmosphere that nearly suffocates the intruder in the meridian heat of our dogdays in those gloomy and horrible swamps!*

---⦾⦾⦾---

JOSEPH MASON

Before he took off to roam the land, Audubon taught French and painting to boys at a Cincinnati school he established. One who answered Audubon's advertisement for students was a widower, the father of a boy who seemed to like to draw. The boy, Joseph Mason, enrolled in Audubon's classes, and soon astonished Audubon by his ability to draw plants—exactly what Audubon needed. He made a deal with Joseph's father. If Joseph could travel with him for a year, Audubon would give him painting lessons.

Before long, Audubon wrote to his wife that Joseph "now draws Flowers better than any man probably in America, though Knowest I do not flatter young artists much. I never said this to him, but I think so." Joseph Mason painted the backgrounds to fifty of the bird portraits in Audubon's famous series The Birds of America.

Joseph [Mason] came and saw it —Shot at it and brought him down." It was the first of several Ivory-bills they would kill that winter. Audubon admired the bird's magnificent spirit even as it was dying: "They sometimes cling to the bark with their claws so firmly, as to remain cramped to the spot for several hours after death."

Later, Audubon withdrew three Ivory-bill specimens from his bag—an adult male, an adult female, and a juvenile male—combed their feathers, and attached thin wires to their wings and limbs. Like a puppeteer he pulled the feathers and toes into dramatic positions that would illustrate the character of these birds. This made them look much more lively and revealing than the stiff poses Alexander Wilson had painted. By manipulating the birds, Audubon could show them in flight, or feeding young, or fluffing up their feathers—whatever seemed most natural. To make sure he got the proportions right, he placed each bird against a wire grid of tiny squares and drew his first sketches on grid paper that had squares of corresponding size. Audubon made three drawings and paintings of the Ivory-bill. The one that became best known showed three woodpeckers vigorously stripping the bark from a dead cypress tree in search of food. As Audubon sketched and painted his specimens and wrote detailed descriptions of the magnificent birds, he seemed to be worrying about the species. Was it doomed? He had seen settlers clear the frontier forests of the Alleghenies and the Ohio Valley, and he must have known that southern trees couldn't be far behind. Of more pressing concern, the Ivory-bill's appearance and behavior made it attractive to hunters and easy to find. Audubon wrote:

[Their calls] are heard so frequently that . . . the bird spends few minutes a day without uttering them; and this circumstance leads to its destruction . . . not because this species is a destroyer of trees but more because it is a beautiful bird, and its rich scalp attached to the upper mandible forms an ornament for the war-dress of most of our Indians, or for the shot-pouch of our squatters and hunters, by all of whom the bird is shot merely for that purpose.

Something about the bill's whiteness made it seem magical to whites and Indians alike. Some Native Americans thought possessing it gave them the bird's mighty power. Mark Catesby, a British naturalist who explored the American South between 1712 and 1725, saw warriors wearing headdresses of white bills strung with "the points outward." The heads were prized objects of trade. "Northern Indians," Catesby wrote, "having none of these birds in their own country, purchase them of the Southern People at the price of two, and sometimes three Buck-skins a bill." Other warriors carried crushed Ivory-bill heads inside their sacred bundles, hoping to inherit the bird's power to drill holes through their enemies. Indians buried the bills with warriors in grave mounds as far away as Colorado—hundreds of miles from the closest Ivory-bill forest.

Audubon also saw "entire belts of Indian chiefs closely ornamented with the tufts and bills of this species." But it wasn't just Indians; everyone wanted the heads and bills. Audubon wrote that frontiersmen were always waiting at steamboat landings, dangling two or three Ivory-bill heads out to disembarking passengers and asking a quarter dollar per head. Some fastened gold chains to the head and upper bill, making watch fobs. Even in European cities, merchants sold dried Ivory-bill skins.

Audubon was clearly concerned about the Ivory-bill's fate, but in the early nineteenth century it was impossible to know for sure how many Ivory-bills were left, or whether the species was in danger of disappearing. During Audubon's lifetime the country was too vast and travel too slow for anyone to keep track of how an entire species was faring. Many bird species hadn't even been named yet, and some had not yet been discovered. There was still a great deal of territory for bird-finders to cover, especially since the area of the United States had doubled in size just a few years before, when President Thomas Jefferson made the Louisiana Purchase from cash-starved France in 1803.

It was even harder to know the status of a species that lived in more than one

SAMPLING THE BIRDS OF AMERICA

For Audubon, knowing a bird often included knowing how it tasted. The Horned Grebe, he said, was fishy, rancid, and fat. The Red-winged Blackbird and the Hermit Thrush were "delicate." The Common Flicker tasted like ants. Bald Eagles reminded him of veal. He didn't describe the taste of an Ivory-billed Woodpecker, though it wouldn't be surprising if he had tried at least one.

country, especially countries separated by water. For while there were also Ivory-billed Woodpeckers in Cuba at the time, hardly anyone in the United States knew it. There would be no mention of the Cuban Ivory-bill in Cuban scientific literature until decades after Audubon's paintings.

Audubon's most famous portrait of the Ivory-bill shows a small family hard at work. The three woodpeckers are charged with energy, sending chips flying through the air, and you can feel the insects beneath the bark scrambling for their lives. The painting captures the spirit of the lordly bird, and shows the respect Audubon had for the Ivory-bill. He may not have been able to count them all, but as he carefully painted his specimens, transferring their colors and lines to paper, he might well have been wondering how long such striking creatures could stay aboard the ark.

The Ivory-bill was so wildly, stunningly beautiful that everywhere Audubon went people seemed to want to give it a distinctive name. Audubon himself called it "the Van Dyke" because its brilliant coloring and bold stripes reminded him of the style of the Flemish portrait artist Anthony Van Dyck. It was "White-back" in northern Florida, "Pate" in western Florida, "Poule de bois" in French southern Louisiana, and "Kent" in northern Louisiana. Seminole Indians called it "Tit-ka." But the most telling nickname of all came from an expression of awe, an exclamation uttered by those who suddenly caught sight of an arrow-like form ripping through the highest leaves of a deep forest, unfolding its three-foot-wide wings to the size of a flag, and then finally swooping straight up to sink its mighty claws into the thick trunk of a cypress tree. At such moments, sometimes all a dumbstruck witness could say was "Lord God, what a bird!"

PLATE 66.

Ivory-billed Woodpecker. Male. 1. F. 2. & 3.
PICUS PRINCIPALIS.

Audubon's painting
of the Ivory-bill in
*The Birds of
America*

Before the
lumber boom of
the late 1870s
there were
millions of acres
of uncut trees in
the South, such
as these longleaf
yellow pines

CHAPTER THREE
"THE ROAD TO WEALTH LEADS THROUGH THE SOUTH"

The South is the bonanza of the future . . . [There are] vast forests untouched, with enormous veins of coal and iron . . . Go South Young Man.

—Businessman Chauncy Depew, in a speech at Yale University, 1894

1885

The Ivory-bill's territory has shrunk. Large areas in the Carolinas and Texas that had once been home to the Ivory-bill are no longer included

Southeastern United States — 1865–1900

THE CIVIL WAR LEFT THE SOUTH A GRAVEYARD OF ASHES AND POVERTY. CLOUDS OF smoke clung to smoldering cities while people in rags foraged for food in the country-side, drifting down dirt roads lined with the bloated carcasses of farm animals the Yankees had shot to starve the Confederates. The war wounded so many people that in 1866 one-fifth of Mississippi's total income was spent on artificial arms and legs. It was nearly impossible to get supplies to southerners, since railroad tracks had been wrenched up into "Sherman's hairpins" so that munitions couldn't move. Bridges lay splintered and rotting at the bottom of rivers.

But the trees that blanketed much of the South remained in place like stoic sen-tinels, sheltering a great variety of plants, snakes, insects, mammals, fishes, and birds, including the Ivory-billed Woodpecker. Even before the Civil War, few southerners had the money or machinery to log the forests and there were few major roads or rail-roads to haul trees to market. When Yankee soldiers came, many plantation families fled for their lives, hastily carving "G.T.T.," or "Gone to Texas," on their walls. Trees began to sprout in the cotton fields they left behind.

After the Civil War a Reconstruction government took over the South, enforced by occupying northern soldiers. The new government sought to guarantee freedom for former slaves, but many southern whites felt it was also out to punish the South for starting and waging the war. Congress passed laws that prohibited southern landowners from selling land at a profit. One such law kept the states of Mississippi, Louisiana, Georgia, and Florida from selling any of their public or unclaimed land, about a third of all the land in those states. As a result, the trees kept growing and dying and regenerating, as they had for thousands of years. If Audubon and Wilson had still been alive to visit the South, they might not have recognized Charleston or Atlanta—much of which lay in ruins—but they would have been right at home in those virgin forests.

Once, the northeastern portion of the United States had also been covered with timber. But after Europeans arrived, pioneer settlers mowed down the trees like an army of termites as they surged west across the country. Most settlers hated the wilderness and feared the creatures who lived within it. The famous Puritan minister Cotton Mather said, "What is not useful is vicious." In other words, if you couldn't use something, it was evil. The first white settlers believed that a cleared patch, neatly fenced off, was a sign of civilization, while a forest left standing was a job undone. And everyone wanted as much land as possible. Trees that weren't used for building were burned as fuel to heat homes and factories, or to run steamboats and railroad engines.

In this fever, many forest creatures of the North began to vanish. Deer, turkeys, and beavers became scarce in many places. Passenger pigeons declined by the millions, and wolves ran out of habitat. By 1800 almost all the original forest east of the Appalachian Mountains had been cleared and settlers were streaming west through the Cumberland Gap or down the Ohio River. Daniel Boone, the famous hunter and Indian fighter, left his home in Kentucky in the 1780s to escape the hot breath of Civilization at his back. Again and again he moved, trying to stay ahead of the forest-clearing blades and torches that always caught up. Schoolchildren sang a song about him:

ENEMY SQUIRRELS

In pioneer days, it was said that there were so many trees in Ohio that a squirrel could travel from the Ohio River to Lake Erie without ever touching the ground. Then settlers made up their minds to rid the land not only of fierce beasts like bears and wolves, but of any other animal that might eat their crops.

In 1807 Ohio passed a law requiring each taxpayer to turn in between ten and one hundred squirrel scalps each year along with his taxes. But in 1822, when even that didn't dent the squirrel population, settlers organized a massive squirrel hunt, killing 19,666 squirrels.

Daniel Boone was ill at ease
When he saw the smoke in the forest trees
There'll be no game in the country soon
"Elbow room!" cried Daniel Boone!

But when Boone revisited Kentucky in 1810, what he found didn't just make him ill at ease. It made him depressed. If ever a place was out of elbow room, it was Kentucky. In despair, he remarked to his friend John James Audubon, "Sir, what a . . . difference thirty years makes in the country! [When I left] you would not have walked out in any direction for more than a mile without shooting a buck or a bear. [But when I returned] a few signs only of deer were to be seen, and as to a deer itself, I saw none."

THE LUMBER BOOM

On October 8, 1871, one of Mrs. Kate O'Leary's five cows kicked over a lantern and set her barn on fire. The flames quickly raced out of control and burned down much of Chicago. So many pine trees around the Great Lakes were cut to rebuild Chicago's houses that by 1880 the *Chicago Tribune* reported that there was only ten years' worth of lumber left in Michigan, Wisconsin, and Minnesota combined. The nation, it warned, was headed for a "timber famine" unless it could change its ways.

But just as the North was running out of wood, a vast new source opened up. Southern politicians regained control of their region in 1877, and the Yankee troops were sent home. Congress cleared the way for southern states to sell their land once again. All at once cash-starved southerners with something to sell—their forested heritage—met wealthy northerners who needed timber. The lumber boom was on.

The fever for southern trees sizzled with the same heat as the Gold Rush of 1849. First, potential investors sent "cruisers" south to find out how big the trees really were and how hard it would be to get them to market. The witnesses came back wide-eyed, thick-tongued, and stammering. There were millions of acres of trees, they said, with crowns that blotted out the sky and trunks thicker around than the combined armspans of two men. Thousands of freed slaves and poor white men were eager to work in the woods for a mere fifty cents a day. The terrain was mostly level and the land dirt cheap. The only catch was that rail lines and roads would have to be built to get men and machines in and logs out.

And so, almost overnight, northern and British investors formed lumber companies. The Illinois Central Railroad arranged for special trains to take land buyers from Chicago to Mississippi. It hired ex–Confederate officers to entertain the lumber brokers with war stories as the miles drifted by. When the stories got old, passengers buried their noses in new books such as *The Road to Wealth Leads Through the South*.

Vast forests changed hands for next to nothing. One northern congressman bought 111,188 acres of Louisiana land in 1876 for less than a dollar an acre. The state of Florida sold 4 million acres to a Philadelphia company in 1881 for only 25 cents an acre. Then a British company bought nearly a million acres in Louisiana for 12 1/2 cents an acre.

Loggers attacked the woods with new machines such as the Barnhart loader pictured here, which allowed logs to be loaded directly onto cars waiting on rails. This is a scene from the 1890s in Laurel, Mississippi

Railroad builders followed the land buyers, clanging out a web of steel. At first the tracks had to be built on nearly level ground, but in 1881 a Michigan lumberman named Ephraim Shay invented a small, powerful locomotive that could chug up and down hills, following the shape of the land. In the 1880s alone, 180 new railroad companies started up east of the Mississippi River. Engines with piercing whistles belched clouds of blue-white steam as they pulled blades and loggers, mules and carts, over the mountains into the pine forests, and later into the swamps.

New tools made it possible to level trees at a furious pace. Woodsmen were given double-bit axes that chewed deeper into bark. The crosscut saw enabled two men to push and pull a long toothed blade back and forth through immense trunks, destroying in an hour what it had taken nature a century to grow. The once silent forest roared with machinery. The fragrance of wet leaves and rain-soaked soil gave way to the scent of tobacco and sawdust, and later of gasoline.

The few men and women who dared to object to the complete destruction of the forests were shouted down as fools. One who spoke up was labeled "immeasurably stupid" by a Chattanooga, Tennessee, newspaper in 1886. "Such stuff, if taken seriously," the paper editorialized, "would leave all nature undisturbed. We welcome the skilled lumberman with his noisy mill."

More and more species of plants, birds, bats, snakes, and mammals ran out of habitat as the wilderness collapsed around them. Ivory-billed Woodpeckers vanished forest by forest and swamp by swamp as the trees were toppled. By 1885 no one could find them at all in North Carolina or northern South Carolina. In 1896 ornithologist Thomas Nuttall warned, "This species is now restricted to the Gulf States and Lower Mississippi Valley." By 1900, the same year a government forestry expert called the leveling of the southern pines "the most rapid and reckless destruction of forests known in history," Ivory-bills became part of Mississippi's history. Fifteen years later, their toy-trumpet call and double-note whacks were gone from Texas, Arkansas, and Alabama, and from most of Florida and Georgia. Retreating deeper into shrinking patches of swamp forest, the few surviving birds became easier to find. They were big, bright, and noisy. And it was their bad luck that, like so many other big, bright, and beautiful things, once they became rare, they also became extremely valuable.

William Brewster collected tens of
thousands of bird specimens and
displayed them in his personal museum

CHAPTER FOUR
TWO COLLECTORS

There is one instance of Ivory-bills apparently disappearing from an area from reasons other than logging, and that is when the Ivory-bills were wiped out of the Suwannee River region of Florida by the collecting of A. T. Wayne in 1892 and 1893.

—James Tanner, *The Ivory-billed Woodpecker* (1942)

South Carolina and Florida — 1892–1894

ARTHUR WAYNE WAS BORN IN CHARLESTON, SOUTH CAROLINA, IN 1863, THE YEAR that Union cannons began a daily bombardment of heavy shells that lasted a year and a half. Wayne's parents fled to the countryside until it was safe to go back. One writer described the Charleston to which they returned in 1865 as "a city of . . . vacant houses, of widowed women, of rotting wharves, of deserted warehouses, of weed-wild gardens, of miles of grass-grown streets."

The Waynes were able to scrape together enough money to educate Arthur until he could go to school. From the very beginning, it was all his teachers could do to keep the slight redheaded boy inside any building at all. He spent as much time as he possibly could hunting birds in the deep green swamps and oatmeal-colored marshes around Charleston, or climbing through the branches of trees looking for nests and eggs. Often he was far beyond reach of the voices that were constantly calling him to "come inside, Arthur, come inside."

But there was one building that seemed to have a tidal pull upon him. It was the Charleston Museum, a few dark rooms at the College of Charleston cluttered with stuffed specimens of plants, animals, birds, and eggs. The oldest museum in the

United States, it was established in 1773, when South Carolina was still a British colony. Later, during the Civil War, as Union general William T. Sherman's troops closed in on Charleston, the museum's staff hastily packed the dead birds and mammals and the jars of insects and frogs into 108 crates, hoisted them onto horse-pulled carts, and shuttled them out to the curator's plantation home in the countryside. Even that almost failed to save them. Union troops swept over the plantation and broke into the building in which the crates were stored. Soldiers pried two of them open. Peering in, they apparently decided that spiders in labeled jars and drawers of stuffed birds posed no danger to the Union.

When Arthur was about ten, he began to go straight from school to the museum nearly every day to help the museum's director, Dr. Gabriel Manigault. Manigault had never met anyone so thirsty for knowledge, especially about birds. The boy never ran out of questions. How could you tell this warbler from that? Why was there no specimen of this or that bird? Soon Wayne was scouring the countryside with his rifle, bringing dead birds back to Dr. Manigault for the museum.

But shooting the bird was only part of the job of creating a museum specimen. The next step was to prepare the specimen so it could exist for eternity in a cabinet or a drawer. This wasn't easy, since the bird had to look real to be of any use to a scholar or to impress a patron. Here Wayne had a wonderful teacher, an elderly British-born curator named John Dancer who had been hired to prepare the museum's specimens. Wayne's apprenticeship began when the two of them went to work on a mockingbird that Wayne had shot and brought in.

Slowly, painstakingly, the old man led Wayne through the tedious steps of taxidermy. First you had to cut open the back of the skull and remove the brains, which, like all internal organs, would rot if left intact. You stuffed the skull with cotton and sewed the skin back up. Then you cut slits into the chest and abdomen of the bird, pushed its legs inside, and pulled the skin off the body as if you were removing a glove, throwing away the flesh and internal organs. Then it was a matter of stuffing the empty skin with cotton to restore the original form of the bird. That was the hardest part. A preparer of specimens had to know the bird really well, as a painter did, to get the proportions right. The most common mistake was putting too much cotton in the chest to puff the bird up and make it look heroic. Finally you sewed the bird back up and combed out the dirt and pellet fragments from the feathers, trying hard to conceal any injuries the shot might have caused.

Most people never find the job that fits their greatest talents. But Arthur T. Wayne found out early in life that he seemed to have been born to collect and prepare birds. He was a keen-eyed observer, able to concentrate so intensely that he could even tell which sex a bird was as it flew in the sky at a great distance. He rarely made a mistake in identifying birds, and was a superb marksman. But good as he was at finding birds and bringing them down, he was even better at preparing specimens. Like a great painter, like an Audubon, Arthur Wayne could bring a bird to life with cotton and a combing brush. Throughout his teen years he collected and put up specimens for his beloved museum, all the while honing his skills.

And yet, after he graduated from high school, life looked like a dead end. He had been an honor student, but his family—like those of most southern high school graduates in the years just after the war—had no money to send

After he decided to devote his life to bird collecting and study, it was said that Arthur T. Wayne rarely even went to the post office without his shotgun

him to college. He had to get a job. And so he did: Arthur T. Wayne, bird genius, began filling out bills of sale in a cotton warehouse like a great musician with no paying concerts. Each day, he counted the hours until he could grab his gun and rush out the door to the field, or hustle to the museum after work. Then, almost by magic, he met the man who would set him free. In the spring of 1883, William Brewster of Massachusetts, one of the best-known bird experts in the United States, arrived in Charleston to visit the museum. Dr. Manigault introduced him to Arthur Wayne, then twenty. Wayne was, as one friend later wrote, "thrilled to the depths of his being."

THE MOST PERFECT MAN

During William Brewster's funeral, one ornithologist remembered him as the most perfect man he ever met. At age thirty-one, when he was introduced to Arthur Wayne, Brewster was a tall, slender, dignified man who dressed with simple taste, moved slowly, and spoke almost poetically.

On the surface, William Brewster and Arthur Wayne had nothing in common. The only child of a wealthy banker, Brewster grew up in a Boston mansion and

Brewster prepares a specimen during a collecting trip along the Suwannee River in 1890

enjoyed a boyhood of riding lessons and private schooling. After he graduated from high school, his father urged him to take up banking, but William resisted. So they struck a bargain: William would give banking an honest try for one year. If he disliked it, his father would drop the matter and never bring it up again. William started at his father's bank as a messenger boy, climbing up the ladder to a management position. When the year was up, he informed his father that his heart just wasn't in the world of finance. And that was the end of banking.

Like Wayne's, Brewster's heart belonged to birds. His father had taught him to shoot a single-barreled shotgun, and a neighbor had given him lessons in stuffing specimens. By the time he visited the Charleston Museum in 1883, William Brewster had been studying and collecting birds for nearly twenty years. He had invested his curious mind, most of his time, and much of his wealth in beginning one of the world's great private collections of bird specimens and eggs. For the first time in his life, Arthur Wayne saw someone he wanted to be like: William Brewster.

Wayne and Brewster hunted birds together nearly every day in the wide swamps and marshes around Charleston during Brewster's visit. Brewster was especially eager to rediscover Swainson's Warbler, a chunky brown-capped songbird that hadn't been seen anywhere for forty years. Early naturalists like Audubon had noted that it was a summer resident in South Carolina, but it was now considered a lost species— maybe even extinct.

Wayne knew in his bones that the warbler was still around and that he could find it. The two men began their search by revisiting the flooded swamps and bamboo thickets where it had last been reported. They spent weeks sloshing about without success. Undaunted, Brewster returned the following spring to search again. On April 22, 1884, Wayne suddenly raised his shotgun to his eye and swung it around to follow a small brown dot. A shot rang out. The bird that fell into the brush turned out to be just what they had hoped—a Swainson's Warbler. A week later Brewster shot another one. Overjoyed, he stayed around Charleston for three more months, during which time the two men killed a total of forty-seven Swainson's Warblers, including several young birds. After Brewster left, Wayne discovered eggs of this species, something no one had ever done before, and proudly wrote about his find in a scientific journal.

As they hunted and prepared their specimens, Brewster and Wayne spent hundreds of hours together talking about birds. Wayne yearned to stop selling cotton and live a life like Brewster's—even though he realized that the Bostonian's independence rested upon an inherited fortune. Brewster encour-

THE PASSENGER PIGEON

Before white settlement, more than one-quarter of all the birds in what is now the United States were Passenger Pigeons. They were so abundant that in 1810 Alexander Wilson saw a flock pass overhead that was a mile wide and 240 miles long, containing over two billion birds. That flock could have stretched nearly twenty-three times around the equator. Passenger Pigeons were pretty and brown, with small grayish heads, barrel chests, and long, tapered wings that sent them through the sky at speeds of up to 60 miles per hour.

But they had two problems: they were good to eat and they destroyed crops by eating seeds. Farmers not only shot them, but also cast huge nets over fields to trap them by the thousands. It took only a few decades to wipe out what may have been the most plentiful bird ever to live on the earth. A fourteen-year-old boy named Press Clay Southworth shot the last wild Passenger Pigeon in 1900. The species became extinct in 1914, when Martha, the last captive pigeon, died quietly in the Cincinnati Zoo.

MARKET HUNTERS

Collectors like Arthur Wayne were usually rough and ingenious outdoorsmen who carried the tools of their trade with them. In hot, humid climates they had to separate the skins from the innards of dead birds right away, or else they would find themselves gagging from the stench of rancid meat and battling swarms of flies. A field collector named Henry Henshaw described what he took with him on a California collecting trip on horseback in 1878:

> *My equipment . . . was simple enough. A pair of roomy saddlebags enabled me to carry a few bottles for the reception of small specimens . . . and a supply of cartridges, cotton, [and] matches. I also carried an insect net attached somewhere about my person, while a good double-barreled shotgun, slung on the horn of the saddle, completed my everyday outfit . . . Two stout boxes, one for supplies such as powder, shot, arsenic, cotton and the like, and the other fitted with trays in which to dry and carry bird and mammal skins, a copper tank of alcohol . . . enclosed in a stout locked box, and a plant press, also [went with me]. My skinning table was improvised by placing one collecting box on top of the other, and a folding stool enabled me to sit down and skin birds with reasonable comfort, although several hours of work usually developed a number of different sorts of backache.*

aged him to try. He needed people like Wayne to provide specimens—birds that would build his collection. Wayne was not only someone who could find the birds he wanted in the South, but someone who could stuff them properly and send them to Boston in good shape. Brewster reminded Wayne that there were also other collectors eager to buy well-preserved specimens and eggs of rare and showy species.

Still, Wayne hesitated to quit his job until he met a second person who set him free. In 1889 Wayne married Maria Porcher, the daughter of a South Carolina plantation family. She dedicated her life to his happiness. The couple settled into a home overlooking a great marsh outside of Charleston, and Arthur Wayne never had to inspect another bale of cotton again.

In the springs of 1892, 1893, and 1894, the Waynes journeyed to Florida so that Arthur could collect rare birds for Brewster and others as well as hunt Manatees for Professor Henry Ward's Natural Science Establishment. By then, Brewster had shifted into a more serious phase of collecting. When his specimens outgrew his family home, he bought three hundred acres of land on the Concord River and built a museum at the rear of his living quarters. He began to buy specimens in larger and larger quantities from all around the country, and hired librarians to help him organize his vast collection. Though Brewster made no promises to Wayne, he was definitely interested in obtaining high-quality Ivory-bill specimens and their eggs. Wayne was confident he could give Brewster exactly what he wanted.

The Waynes arrived in Branford, Florida, on the Suwannee River, in March 1892. After setting up his collecting table, Arthur went out to find men to help him. He asked around for local hunters and trappers who knew the countryside, letting it be known that he would pay four to five dollars per skin for Ivory-billed Woodpeckers in good condition.

Away from home for the first time, the Waynes found themselves living in poverty, depending on payments from bird buyers that came in the mail. Brewster was slow to pay. Sometimes months passed between the time Wayne sent off specimens to Boston and the time he received Brewster's replies, which didn't always contain money.

On September 16, 1892, Wayne wrote Brewster in desperation, "On the Suwannee River from March to August . . . I secured thirteen [Ivory-billed Woodpecker] specimens, and have sold all but the finest . . . Will you advance me $25.00 on the trip and I will give you the refusal of all the birds I get?"

But Brewster didn't advance the money, and the Waynes were forced to return to South Carolina for the winter. They were back in Florida the next spring, hunting in the Orlando area for Carolina Parakeets and more Ivory-bills. The Ivory-bill was the star attraction, fetching a far higher price than any other species.

Though he shot some birds himself, Wayne mainly depended on keen-eyed strangers to bring him specimens. He called these collectors "country crackers," and was constantly worried that they would deliver Ivory-bills with cracked or chipped bills, or damaged feathers. Wayne also had to compete with other collectors. He fumed about his chief rival, W.E.D. Scott, who also collected in Florida. "Mr Scott did not secure one Paroquet [the soon-to-be-extinct Carolina Parakeet] on his last collecting trip to Florida!" Wayne reminded Brewster. "No one has taken as many Paroquets as I have in the same space of time. Neither has anyone taken as many Ivory-bills, or Bachman's

WARD'S NATURAL SCIENCE ESTABLISHMENT

Who else but Professor Henry Ward had traveled around the world seven times, sat atop Mount Sinai, and survived smallpox? Henry Ward ran away from home at the age of twelve and never quit exploring. Sent to Europe at twenty to tutor a friend, he went on to Egypt to collect fossils, skins, and artifacts.

Returning to his hometown of Rochester, New York, he began to buy and sell massive quantities of skins, skeletons, eggs, and specimens. He filled many a private cabinet (as well as college collections) with his specimens. His headquarters, Ward's Natural Science Establishment, was founded in Rochester in 1862. Packed into his headquarters were colossal exhibits including Jumbo, P. T. Barnum's circus elephant, who had been hit by a locomotive— his skeleton is shown below.

Not only was Ward's a popular tourist destination, it was a huge marketplace for collectors. That's why Arthur Wayne was eager to help satisfy Professor Ward's interest in adding the Florida Manatee to his establishment.

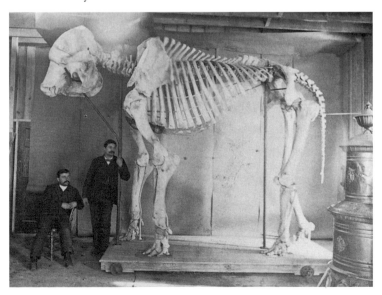

Ivory-billed Woodpecker, male	
and female	*$22.00*
Mississippi Kite, price reduced	*2.00*
4 Carolina Paroquets, adults	*15.00*
1 (Carolina) Paroquets, immature	*3.50*
3 South Carolina Swifts @ .50	*1.50*
1 Scott's Sparrow	*1.25*
1 Red-eyed Vireo	*.25*
1 Yellow-throated Vireo	*.30*
1 Acadian Flycatcher	*.35*
1 Bachman's Warbler	*2.50*
1 Parula Warbler, Blue Head	*1.00*
1 Black-poll Warbler	*.25*
1 Worm-eating Warbler	*.50*
4 Manau's Marsh Wrens	*3.20*
Total	*53.60*

warblers. I do not mean to brag, but my success is due to the interest I take."

All in all, Wayne's field journals show that he killed or paid for the killing of forty-four Ivory-billed Woodpeckers in Florida between 1892 and 1894. According to researcher James Tanner, who interviewed some of Wayne's "country crackers" in the 1930s, Wayne's work all but eliminated the Ivory-bill along three Florida rivers. Of these birds, Brewster bought only seven, paying an average of about twelve dollars per bird. Brewster also bought fifty-four specimens from other collectors, eventually giving him one of the largest collections of Ivory-bill specimens in the world.

WHAT'S HIT IS HISTORY

Why did Arthur Wayne need to kill forty-four Ivory-billed Woodpeckers, and why did William Brewster need to buy sixty-one specimens? Didn't they realize the bird was nearing extinction? If so, didn't they care?

Of course they knew Ivory-bills were rare—that's what made them valuable. Wealthy collectors like Brewster competed fiercely to buy the few specimens of rare and almost extinct birds. Brewster was both a scientist and a collector—during the late 1800s there wasn't always a clear distinction between the two. As a scientist, he wanted a large number of specimens to study all the variations found in birds of different sexes and ages, and from different parts of their range. Males and females look different in most species, as do juveniles and adults, as do birds in, say, the northern extreme of where they live compared to those in southern locations. To really understand a species as a whole, it's important to observe these differences, and to try to understand what they mean to the birds themselves.

William Brewster wrote a great deal about birds and made valuable scientific contributions to ornithology. So did Arthur Wayne: he discovered many new species in South Carolina and wrote the first field guide to the birds of South Carolina, still considered a masterpiece of detail. And in those days, before cameras, an assortment of field guides, and binoculars, the most reliable way to study birds was to kill them and examine them closely. Without specimens, we would not have the foundation of knowledge upon which ornithology rests. Collecting was a big part of what ornithologists did.

But the question still remains: Why did they need so many? If people like Brewster and Wayne knew so much and cared so much about birds, wouldn't they have wanted to keep a species like the Ivory-bill alive at all costs? Maybe. Neither man knew for sure how many Ivory-bills were left, since there was still no way to make a reliable count of all the individual birds within a species' range.

Neither man seemed willing or able to believe that his actions could be contributing to the demise of the Ivory-bill. When Wayne wrote about the Ivory-bill's disappearance on the Wacissa River in Florida, he blamed it on the men he was paying to kill them. "This magnificent bird was once very common in this region," Wayne wrote, ". . . but it is now rapidly becoming extinct on the Wacissa . . . They are shot for food, and the people—the crackers—consider them better than ducks!"

Extinction was not a big topic when Brewster and Wayne were collecting. When whites first settled North America, many believed there were so many birds that it was impossible to completely destroy a species. By the time of Brewster and Wayne, scientists knew that the Great Auk and the Heath Hen and the Labrador Duck were gone and that others might soon follow. A few scientists and collectors were beginning to think about the danger their work posed. "The true ornithologist goes out to study birds alive and destroys some of them simply because that is the only way of learning their structure and technical characters," wrote ornithologist Elliott Coues in 1890. But his was a rare voice. Even those who noticed that particular birds were missing were not thinking about protecting the

CABINETS AND PRIVATE MUSEUMS

"This bird is not at all abundant," wrote one collector of the Ivory-bill in 1879, "and specimens may be regarded as good additions to one's cabinet." By "cabinet" the writer meant the grandfather-clock-sized cases with glass windows that loomed in the parlors of the wealthy throughout America and Europe during Victorian times. They were jammed with stuffed birds clinging to dried vegetation, dried butterflies, decorative stones, seashells, dead beetles, birds' eggs and nests, and even stuffed frogs.

A few extremely wealthy collectors like William Brewster built huge personal museums, collecting tens of thousands of dead birds, which were stuffed and exhibited. Brewster had 40,000 skins when he died, the second-largest collection in North America. He willed it to Harvard University, where it is now part of Harvard's Museum of Comparative Zoology. Like all collectors, these men and women bought multiple specimens of the same species to trade with other museums.

In Brewster's day, the largest collection in the world was owned by Lord Rothschild of Tring, England, a fabulously wealthy man who personally owned more than 300,000 bird skins and mounts by the time he died in 1937.

habitat for endangered species. And there was little understanding of the role that any one species played within an entire ecosystem. Bird experts were still fixed on collecting, stuffing, studying, and writing about species. As many put it, "What's hit is history, what's missed is mystery."

Those who traded in rare birds probably didn't want to know that their work was pushing a bird toward extinction. Ivory-billed Woodpeckers meant money to Arthur Wayne and prestige to William Brewster. Wayne was able to sell his Ivory-bills for about ten dollars on average. He had to pay his "crackers" four or five dollars per bird, so if he either bought or killed forty-four birds, he might have made at least three hundred dollars, minus the cost of his supplies and his travel to and from Florida. It wasn't a fortune even then, but it meant a lot to Wayne, who desperately wanted to view himself as a professional ornithologist.

Special Collections of
BIRDS' EGGS
At Unheard of Prices to Close Out.

All specimens are first class, side-blown, true to name. Safe delivery guaranteed.

Collection No 1 Contains:

Wood Ibis, Great Blue Heron, Snowy Heron, Black-crowned Night Heron, Green Heron, American Coot, Lapwing, Killdeer, Bob-white, Florida Burrowing Owl, Flicker, American

Collectors took eggs from nests and removed the contents with a straw. Egg prices were listed in catalogues such as "The Oologist" (meaning one who studies eggs)

In the end, no matter what damage their work did to a particular species, the collectors kept collecting because they loved to. As one writer put it, "Collecting provided a convenient and socially acceptable excuse for respectable grown men to climb trees, scramble down cliffs, go camping and roam freely out of doors."

Arthur Wayne and William Brewster: bird scholars, bird shooters, bird traders. Collectors. As leaders in the field of ornithology, they asked many important questions. But while Wayne stuffed the big black-and-white skins with cotton and Brewster packed his cabinets full of well-formed specimens, one question they never seemed to ask was "Is there still time for the Ivory-billed Woodpecker?"

The widespread use of feathers on ladies' hats—or even of whole birds, as seen here—sparked the Plume War

CHAPTER FIVE
THE PLUME WAR

A bird in the bush is worth two in the hand.

—Motto adopted in 1899 by *Bird-Lore*, which became the official magazine of the

National Association of Audubon Societies of North America

In the early twentieth century ancient trees were cut out of swamps, crowding the Ivory-bill into smaller forests, widely separated from each other

Marshes and Swamps of the U.S.A. and Beyond—1870–1920

FEW WOMEN OUT WINDOW-SHOPPING IN NEW YORK CITY ON A WARM SPRING DAY in 1887 noticed the square-faced, bespectacled man strolling slowly behind them, pausing every now and then to scribble something down in a notebook. Those who did might have found it curious that his eyes rarely wandered below the tops of their heads. The man was Frank Chapman, an ornithologist for the American Museum of Natural History, and in some ways he was doing what he often did: counting birds.

But this was the most disturbing bird tally he had ever done. Chapman wanted to see for himself just how far the plumed hat fashion craze had gone. After two blocks of strolling, he walked briskly back to his office and compiled the grim statistics: he had seen 700 hats, of which 542 had feathers sewn into them. There were feathers from forty different species, including woodpeckers, bluebirds, flycatchers, owls, herons, and warblers. Some of the hat brims were like small tabletops, holding up great heaps of feathers. And it wasn't just feathers: one of the spring's most admired styles contained the beak, claws, and legs of a dead crow. Something had to be done.

Frank Chapman became a key soldier in the "Plume War," a struggle to keep birds from being slaughtered so that hats could be decorated with their feathers, or "plumes." The war lasted nearly fifty years. During this time, passions boiled, fortunes changed hands, and men were even killed. Out of this bitter fight came America's first conservation groups, including the Audubon Society, which later took the lead in trying to save the Ivory-billed Woodpecker. The Plume War also gave birth to strong bird protection laws and created the first nature preserves for birds. Perhaps most important, during this time millions of American schoolchildren fished dimes out of their pockets and became Junior Audubon members, learning to study and protect birds rather than shoot them. There may not have been uniformed soldiers in the Plume War, but plenty of blood was shed and millions of lives were lost.

FEATHERED GOLD

For centuries a plume sticking out of one's hat had been a jaunty mark of distinction in Europe. Napoleon wore a plume. So did fictional characters like the Three Muske-

A Snowy Egret

teers, Captain Hook, and Cyrano de Bergerac. Around 1850, European women began to wear plumed hats, too, and by about 1870, the fashion trend had taken such a powerful hold in the United States that many American women wouldn't think of buying a hat that wasn't topped by at least one long bird feather.

Suddenly there was even more money to be made from bird carcasses than could be earned by shooting specimens to stock museums or specimen cabinets. Milliners—hatmakers—were paying high prices to hunters who would gun down brightly colored birds, strip the feathers from their carcasses, and pack the feathers into bales for shipment to Europe or New York. By 1900, one of every eighty-three Americans was employed in the hatmaking business. Three years later, an ounce of plumes—requiring the death of four birds—was worth twice as much as an ounce of gold.

The most valuable feathers of all were produced by two tall, long-legged wading birds called the Great Egret and the Snowy Egret. During their spring breeding seasons, their plumes, called "aigrettes," were long, silky, and elegant, extending from the bird's shoulders to its feet. Especially when aigrettes started selling for a dollar a feather, plume hunters slipped into rookeries (clusters of heron and egret nests) and opened fire. Most adult birds remained with their eggs and nestlings instead of flying to safety. Stories of massacres soon reached the nation's newspapers. One witness wrote, "Here and there in the mud lay the lifeless forms of eight of the birds. They had been shot down and the skin bearing the plumes stripped from their backs. Flies were busily at work . . . In four of the nests young orphan birds could be seen who were clamoring piteously for food which their dead parents would never again bring to them."

On a January day in 1896, a bird-loving Boston woman decided she had read one such story too many. Harriet Hemenway was wealthy, well connected, and born to lead. She took her well-worn copy of the *Boston Blue Book*—a directory of Boston's wealthy and elite citizens—and began to thumb through it with her cousin Minna Hall. "We marked the ladies

CHRISTMAS BIRD COUNTS

In 1900, Audubon leader Frank Chapman proposed "a new kind of Christmas side hunt in the form of a Christmas Bird Census." He asked that all readers of Bird-Lore *magazine spend part of Christmas Day counting the birds around them and sending in a report of which species they saw and how many of each they counted. Twenty-seven people went out that day, reporting ninety species.*

A century later, the Christmas Bird Count still continues, with more than fifteen hundred counts going on throughout the United States, Canada, and a few other countries. Many thousands of people take part, recording what amounts to a giant snapshot of how birds are doing on that particular day. With over one hundred years of records, the counters can show whether a particular species is increasing, decreasing, or staying steady over time. And they have a lot of fun. Counters have recorded as many as 350 species near the Panama Canal, and as few as one—the Common Raven—at Prudhoe Bay, Alaska.

of fashion who would be likely to wear aigrettes on their hats or in their hair," Minna Hall later wrote. "We then sent out circulars asking the women to join a society for the protection of birds, especially the egret. Some women joined and some who preferred to wear the feathers would not join."

Hemenway and Hall called their new organization the Massachusetts Audubon Society. Audubon chapters began to spring up in state after state as concern for plumed birds spread. Frank Chapman started a magazine called *Bird-Lore* for the

The winners of an Audubon-sponsored birdhouse design contest in 1917 show off their entries

Audubon Societies, with each issue including articles for children. Thousands of children joined Junior Audubon Clubs, learning to draw and paint birds and then plunging into the fields and woods to study them in real life. Some got free memberships but only if they signed a pledge card saying "I promise not to harm our birds or their eggs, and to protect them both whenever I am able."

In 1905, state Audubon chapters became even stronger by forming the National Association of Audubon Societies, with headquarters in New York City. Leaders gave public lectures, often blaming the Plume War more on the women who bought plumed hats than on the hunters who killed and sold the birds or the milliners who bought them.

The Audubon Societies pushed bird protection laws through legislatures in state after state, and followed up by hiring armed wardens to patrol the rookeries. But with plumed hats still in style, there was always money to be made, and hunters continued to blast away. Hunters and armed wardens circled each other warily in the last few great rookeries. With so much at stake, a showdown was inevitable.

MURDER AT CUTHBERT LAKE

Heretofore the price has been the life of the birds, now is added human blood.
—*Bird-Lore* magazine, 1905

One desolate, mosquito-infested patch of south Florida is remembered as the Gettysburg of the Plume War. Cuthbert Lake was a shallow pond fringed by a tangle of

Plume hunters display their bounty

mangrove trees, set deep in the Everglades. It had been named for a plume hunter who, as legend had it, had followed a drifting white feather into the Everglades until it led him to a giant rookery hidden deep in a mangrove swamp. When he pushed aside the last branches and beheld the multitude of wading birds before him, his eyes widened like those of a gold prospector who had seined a nugget in his pan. Cuthbert raised his rifle and shot until his ammunition gave out.

When Florida passed a bird protection law in 1901, the president of the organization later called the National Audubon Society hired rugged, sunburned Guy Bradley to defend the last big rookeries in the Florida Keys. Bradley knew the Keys, and he knew many of the plume hunters personally since he himself had grown up hunting birds for pay. At the age of sixteen he, with his brother Louis and three friends, had sailed around the tip of Florida, collecting birds for a Miami taxidermist known as "the Frenchman." He had had the time of his life back then, but now, at thirty-five, Bradley had soured on the plume trade. Anyone could see that there were many fewer birds now, and yet the hunters snickered at the new law. When Audubon's president offered thirty-five dollars a week for a warden's position, Bradley didn't hesitate. He knew it was dangerous, but he had two young boys to feed—and he believed in the work.

One of his first acts was to arrest several men he knew well. Suddenly old friends lowered their voices when he walked into a room. Then, on the morning of July 8, 1905, a Saturday, Bradley squinted out from the front porch of his cottage at the tip of the Everglades and saw a white sailboat heading across Florida Bay toward Cuthbert Lake. He scrambled to the shore, pushed his own small rowboat into the water, and took off after it. That was the last anyone saw of Guy Bradley. A few days later, a pair of boaters, curious about the vultures hovering above what appeared to be an empty rowboat, discovered Bradley's bullet-riddled body inside. Plume hunters were arrested for Bradley's murder but were soon released.

Two more Audubon wardens were murdered not long afterward. Public opinion swung sharply against the plume hunters and in favor of the Audubon Society. More and more women refused to buy feathered hats and pressured their friends to do the same. President Theodore Roosevelt threw his weight behind the Audubon movement, helping to close down the factories where birds were made into skins. There were victories in the swamps, too: in 1909 wardens finally tracked down the elusive plume hunter Arthur Lambert, a mastermind at staying one step ahead of the law. Once, Lambert had escaped officers by leaping from a boat into the Sampit River and swimming underwater to the other side, melting like an otter into the reeds along the far bank. Lambert

THE BOB

A new hairstyle helped end the Plume War. In 1914, actress and famed dancer Irene Castle appeared in a show with her hair cut short and blunt. She called it a "bobbed" cut. She had cut her hair to prepare for an appendectomy, and it hadn't had time to grow back for her performance. It didn't matter: her new look caught on immediately. Soon acres of hair were piled up on beauty parlor floors. Bobbed hair made heads too small to hold up the huge, tabletop-sized hats that had been loaded down with bird feathers. Demand for feathers lessened as the "bob" took over.

was later arrested when wardens, acting on a tip, flung open the lid of a steamer trunk and trained their pistols on him.

In 1910, New York outlawed the sale or possession of feathers from protected species, including herons and egrets. It was a major victory for the Audubon movement, since most of the country's hatmakers operated out of New York City, but it came almost too late. That same year, scientists estimated that there were only about 1,400 Great Egrets and 250 Snowy Egrets left in the world.

Three years later, the U.S. Congress prohibited anyone from bringing into the United States the "feathers, quills, heads, wings, tails, skins or parts of skins of wild birds . . . except for scientific or educational purposes." Soon elegant ladies stepped off ocean liners fresh from buying sprees in Paris or London, only to be greeted by polite U.S. customs agents who flashed badges and took their hats away.

ROGER TORY PETERSON'S FAMOUS BOOK

By the time he was twenty-six, Roger Tory Peterson (shown here as an older man) had painted pictures of every bird species found in the eastern United States. Then he set out to collect his bird portraits into a single pocket-sized book that could help amateur bird-watchers tell the species apart.

Five publishing companies turned him down before Houghton Mifflin published his work as A Field Guide to the Birds. *The book sold out in one week. It popularized bird-watching by pointing out simple ways of identifying birds and became one of the most important books of the twentieth century.*

"DOC"

As the Plume War raged, American students studied the bird pictures that came with their Junior Audubon membership kits, and roamed the countryside looking for birds. One of these students, Roger Tory Peterson, got his kit in 1919 when he was an eleven-year-old seventh-grader in Jamestown, New York. It cost a dime, and it seemed like a waste of money until one day, in school, he started painting a picture of a Blue Jay. Something about the colors sparked his imagination.

He was still thinking about this the next Saturday when he and a friend went exploring. They had just crested a hill when Roger spotted a clump of brown feathers clinging to the trunk of an oak tree. The object looked dead, but somehow it was still attached to the tree. Puzzled, Roger walked up to it, extended his finger, and touched it. "It came instantly to life," he later wrote, "looked at me with wild eyes and dashed away in a flash of golden wings." It was a Common Flicker, a kind of woodpecker, sleeping with its face tucked into the feathers of its back. That single moment changed Roger Peterson's whole life. "Ever since," he later wrote, "birds have seemed to me the most vivid expression of life. They have dominated my daily thoughts, my reading and even my dreams."

Millions of children soaked up information about birds from the pages of Audubon's *Bird-Lore*. For many students, the best part in the whole magazine was the bird biography. *"I am the Golden Plover,"* it would begin, and would go on to describe in the bird's imaginary voice how it found food, attracted mates, raised its young, and navigated its way on its long migratory flights. Every issue featured a different bird.

The stories were written by Professor Arthur Augustus Allen of Cornell University, a world expert in bird behavior. "Doc," as his ornithology students called him, shared his home with his wife, Edna—also an ornithologist—their five children, one Burrowing Owl, a free-roaming crow, a family of Rose-breasted Grosbeaks, and dozens of wild ducks who bathed in the pond behind the house.

And always there were special guests. One was a young Golden Eagle that a farmer had captured and delivered to Doc's office at Cornell. Doc brought it home and put it in a pen outside. For fifteen days the great bird refused all offers of food. It turned its beak away from dead mice, scorned dead rabbits, and ignored dead chickens—it even declined fresh fish. Finally, remembering that eagles kill most of their food themselves, Doc pushed a live black hen into the pen and shut the

THE BRONX COUNTY BIRD CLUB

In the late 1920s nine intensely competitive boys and young men—including Roger Tory Peterson—raced around the five boroughs of New York City, tracking down rare birds and learning together how to identify them. Calling themselves the Bronx County Bird Club (BCBC), they turned bird-watching into a sport. From their clubhouse near the Harlem River, they issued challenges to other teams of birders around New York City to see who could find the most birds in twenty-four hours.

Using maps, binoculars, and coordinated strategies, they prepared for birding contests as if they were going to war. They especially loved to show up older bird-watchers from clubs around New York City. While their elders were stuck at their jobs, the boys got out of school in midafternoon and used the hours to survey the contest area in advance. One of their favorite sites was a dump in the Bronx where they once discovered four Snowy Owls feeding on rats.

The BCBC was rarely beaten.

door. The two birds looked at each other and went to sleep side by side. The eagle soon gave up its hunger strike and ate whatever Doc gave it, but it would never touch its companion, the hen. Wondering if the eagle was no longer a predator—a killer of live food—Doc shoved in another hen. The door had scarcely shut before the eagle pounced on and devoured the newcomer.

Professor Allen was always experimenting with new equipment, too, especially cameras and recording devices. In the spring of 1924, he and Edna stuffed their cameras, lenses, film canisters, and binoculars into a Model T Ford and headed south to photograph and film some of America's rarest birds. When they reached Florida they were introduced to a lean, leather-faced guide named Morgan Tindall, who said he could lead them to a pair of Ivory-billed Woodpeckers.

The Allens leaped at the chance. The Ivory-billed Woodpecker hadn't been reported for years, and many ornithologists assumed it was extinct. But suppose it wasn't—what a find that

BINOCULARS

The need to shoot specimens lessened as it became possible to fit powerful magnifying lenses into binoculars. At first, only the wealthy could afford them, but by the 1920s even the youthful members of the Bronx County Bird Club were able to afford seven dollars each to buy mail-order binoculars that could make birds look four times their actual size. Today, lightweight binoculars can magnify images forty times and more.

would be! With Tindall shouting directions over the engine's rumble, the Allens gunned the car through flooded swamps. Sheets of gray moss hung from giant, widely spaced cypress trees. For seventeen long miles the Ford's wheels were completely underwater. One evening the engine sputtered to a stop and refused to restart. Miles from help, the Ford became an island in an alligator-infested swamp. To the Allens' great relief, it roared to life again the next morning.

Tindall was right about the Ivory-bills. Just after dawn on April 12, Doc Allen peeked out from a crouched position behind a blind made of palmetto leaves, and saw two huge black-and-white woodpeckers winging through the cypress trees. Clearly showing a broad saddle of white on the lower wings, they swooped up and came to rest high on a dead pine snag. When Allen could steady his fingers, he pointed, not a shotgun, but a camera at the birds, and snapped history's first photographs of Ivory-billed Woodpeckers.

The birds called a few times and then flew off together back into the swamp. Allen sloshed frantically after them, then gave up to catch his breath and empty his boots. But that evening the birds returned, and they came again the next day, finally leading the explorers to a dead cypress tree with a twisted snag of a top. Thirty feet above the ground was a large, freshly chiseled oval cavity. It was a nest—that meant the Ivory-bills were still reproducing. Allen got more clear photographs and was able to describe the Ivory-bills' courtship, though he had to leave before young birds were hatched.

The sensational discovery made headlines throughout the country. Reporters turned the scholarly Allens into safari heroes. One newspaper called their trip "an expedition fraught with peril and adventure, penetrating far into the disease-infested glades of Florida in search of rare forms of bird life." Headlines trumpeted, "CORNELL EXPERTS FIND BIRDS WITH BILLS OF IVORY" and "RARE FEATHERED FREAKS REVEALED IN UN-EXPLORED FLORIDA SWAMPS."

More important, Doc Allen came back to Cornell with nearly seven thousand photographs and 1,600 feet of motion-picture film of birds that few Americans had seen. He had added to America's knowledge of birds without ever firing a shot. And, of course, he had rediscovered the Ivory-billed Woodpecker. But just before he and Edna left Florida, a message from Tindall cast the whole expedition into a cloud of gloom. Two local collectors had been following the Allens and Tindall on their Florida quest. They knew the Ivory-bills were valuable and had asked the county sheriff for a permit to hunt them. Amazingly, the sheriff had obliged. Now, according to Morgan Tindall, the birds were gone.

So it was that the normally unflappable Arthur Allen wore a grim expression when he gave reporters a terse statement: "As long as the state of Florida allows [Ivory-bills] to be taken legally," he said, ". . . the species is doomed to certain extinction." He didn't share his personal feelings, but he must have worried that their extinction might have already occurred. Worst of all must have been the thought that he, Arthur Allen, America's only full-time professor of ornithology and a man who had dedicated his life to understanding birds in the wild, had unwittingly helped to seal the fate of America's rarest bird.

The first photograph ever taken—by Doc Allen—of the Ivory-billed Woodpecker

CHAPTER SIX
LEARNING TO THINK LIKE A BIRD

My best Acquaintances are those
With Whom I spoke no Word.

—Emily Dickinson

Central New York State — 1914–1934

THERE IS A FAMILY PHOTOGRAPH OF JIMMY TANNER, EIGHT OR NINE YEARS OLD, SEATED on a park bench, looking out at the world through a pair of binoculars. Beside him, his tall older brother, Edward, is bent in intense concentration over a book while his mother also reads. Jimmy is in a world of his own, totally absorbed in whatever he is looking at. Odds are it was a bird.

The slender, sandy-haired boy behind the binoculars would grow up to become forever linked to the Ivory-billed Woodpecker. He would know it best, spend the most time with it, record its voice, take the best pictures of it, and devote years of his life to trying to save it from extinction. Had he been born a few decades earlier, he might well have grown up, like Arthur Wayne, trying to study the Ivory-bill by collecting specimens. But he was a product of the Audubon movement, part of the first generation of ornithologists that learned mainly by studying how birds behaved in their natural habitats.

Jim Tanner was born in the small town of Cortland, New York, in 1914, the same year that Martha, the last Passenger Pigeon, died in the Cincinnati Zoo. The Tanners gave their two sons a well-rounded education that included a strenuous outdoor life, a church upbringing, and exposure to mechanical skills as well as book learning. Jim could fix almost anything and invent what he couldn't. He could take complicated things apart, remember where he had laid all the pieces, and then put them back together. People told him that if he could ever think of anything useful to invent, he might get rich someday. To make themselves hardier, like President Theodore Roosevelt, Jim and Edward slept outside on a screened-in porch even on the frostiest New York winter nights. They shivered plenty, but rarely got sick.

More than anything Jim loved the outdoors. He explored the territory near his home after school, seldom making it home "by dinner," the family rule. On weekends he set off on long hikes, stuffing a slab of beef wrapped in waxed paper into his knapsack to cook over a fire when he got hungry. Sometimes alone, sometimes with his friend Carl McAllister, he traced the flat, low ridges around the lake country of central New York, exploring the gorges and blue glacial ponds, hauling himself up granite boulders, probing through marshes, learning to be quieter.

Like most small-town boys, Jim owned a rifle and liked to shoot it, but he never took it with him. He even refused to collect butterflies with his friends because he couldn't make himself stick pins in their wings. He wanted to meet wild things on their own terms, not his.

All nature was interesting to Jim, but nothing was as fascinating as birds. He especially loved to listen to them. He practiced imitating their songs and could sometimes get them to answer him. He taught himself which birds sang from the ground, which sounded from the middle of trees, and which called from the highest branches. He got so that he could even tell them apart by their one-note chips—sharp little warning notes which had no melody. He learned to identify nests and eggs. He picked up owl pellets—regurgitated wads of matter that owls couldn't digest—from under pine trees and used a twig to tease tiny mouse bones from the fur balls. Sometimes he hiked with a heavy camera, snapping pictures that he developed when he got home, turning the family bathroom into a darkroom.

Jim learned a lot from school, but his most valuable lessons came on those long hikes. He kept a journal, starting with the date and time of day and noting the weather and the direction of the wind. He made himself go a long time between meals. He learned to sit still against a tree even if the bark was digging into his shoulder blades and itching like mad. Most important, he learned that while you can't meet wildlife by appointment, if you study wild creatures carefully enough, you can predict where they will be.

By the time Jim was a teenager, he had sailed through his scout badge on ornithology and was known as a town expert on birds. When someone picked up a wounded Golden Eagle far out of its range, he naturally took it to Jim. Jim kept it in a cage in his home and fed it rodents until it regained its strength. Then, like a falconer, he taught it how to hunt from his arm.

Jim Tanner with the Golden Eagle he rescued

As Jim Tanner entered his senior year of high school, he had many possibilities to choose from, but he had plans of his own. By the greatest stroke of luck, he lived only twenty-two miles from Cornell University, one of the world's premier centers of bird knowledge, where Professor Arthur Augustus Allen offered America's sole course of study in ornithology. That meant that Jim was only an hour's bus ride away from a chance to make his living learning about, teaching about, and helping birds. Ranked third in his class, he applied to Cornell and was quickly accepted.

By the time he said goodbye to his family in the late summer of 1931, Jim Tanner was almost as much a creature of the forest as any songbird, and as hungry for knowledge as an owl for a mouse. At last he was headed to Ithaca, New York, to study with the world-famous Dr. Allen at Cornell. No more "be home by dinner" for him. From now on, dinner would be whenever he could find time to eat.

OLD MCGRAW

The center of every Cornell ornithology student's universe was McGraw Hall. When people stepped into the creaky building from the often snow-covered campus, their eyes had to suddenly adjust to the dim light even as their nostrils filled with the sharp odor of formaldehyde. Jammed into McGraw's three noisy floors were dozens of small classrooms, offices, closets, and even a museum. Bird skeletons raised their wing bones from dusty windowsills. Stuffed hawks and owls and shorebirds stared silently from every nook and cranny. Pickled bird parts floated lazily in briny jars that rested on shelves in laboratory rooms.

Bird students investigated and experimented all day and all night. Many projects involved getting to know more about what birds ate. Live bullfrogs splashed in McGraw's sinks, and field mice scraped their claws against the slick sides of big tubs kept in the lab rooms. There were refrigerators containing

---

THE ROUGHING-OUT ROOM AT MCGRAW

If you want to learn about birds, you have to get to know bugs, since birds of almost every family eat insects and spiders. At McGraw, the "Roughing-Out Room" high in a drafty tower of the old building was the place where students took notes as hordes of beetles attacked the crudely skinned corpses of birds and animals, breaking them down into skeletons which were then studied further.

Cornell professor George Sutton wrote: "In the roughing-out room, the fumes of ammonia are so strong as to be all but overpowering. Had Edgar Allan Poe spent two minutes in this chamber of horrors, he might have written a mystery thriller the likes of which are not on the world's bookshelves today."

Doc Allen oversees a Cornell ornithology class at McGraw Hall. Note the bird skeletons on the windowsill

dead cats, and gunnysacks stuffed with dead hawks and owls whose stomachs awaited examination. One student even had his own collection of snakes, at least until the day they all got loose. For months afterward, bloodcurdling screams rang out through the building. After a while, students didn't even notice. Screams only meant that someone had encountered a Blue Racer coiled behind a specimen flask, or maybe that a blacksnake had dropped onto a student's open textbook from a library shelf above.

In 1931, the Great Depression created widespread poverty and made it hard for many families to send their children to college. Doc Allen did everything he could to keep his bird students in school, including letting a few of them live at McGraw. One young man from Florida, having no money to rent a room, unrolled his mattress each night on top of a long classroom laboratory table and fell asleep. The students who opened the door for early-morning lectures sometimes startled him awake, causing him to scramble into his trousers and dive behind a cabinet to shave. He cooked his dinner—usually a stew of carrots, beans, and bread crusts—in a big pot, adding the bodies of whatever Red Squirrels and chipmunks he was able to trap on campus that day.

Jim Tanner, with financial help from his family, moved his belongings into an all-male rooming house which provided a bed and dinner for five dollars a week. It was all he needed. For Tanner and his fellow ornithology students it was birds, birds, birds, almost twenty-four hours a day. He took classes in entomology (the study of insects), zoology, and German, a language in which many articles about birds were written. He also studied drawing, bacteriology, botany, and genetics. He especially liked Professor Allen's new course, "Conservation of Wildlife," which explored how to preserve wild species in their natural habitats. It was the first such course in the United States.

Every Monday night, Tanner stomped into McGraw with his classmates, his professors, and invited guests for the week's discussion on birds. The seminar sessions began with each person telling the entire group about the birds he or she had seen on campus in the past week. It was a chance to shine before the others, or to make an embarrassing mistake out loud. Doc, who led the group, never reacted to errors in bird identification with laughter or harsh words, but instead with gentle questioning and thoughtful remarks, which could be even worse. A student named Sally Hoyt Spofford remembers reporting a Swamp Sparrow in March, far too early for the bird to be in Ithaca. The others looked down at their boots and tried to conceal smiles as Sally's face reddened. "How interesting," Dr. Allen mused, his voice light. "That *is* an early one."

Tanner pushed himself hard, learned rapidly, and won high marks. He flew through a four-year course in just three years. In the spring of 1934, when he was finishing his undergraduate studies and wondering what to do next, McGraw was buzzing with rumors and wagers about how Doc was going to spend his sabbatical leave. Doc had taught at Cornell for more than twenty years without a long break. In that time, he had made Cornell a world leader in the study of birds. At last he was going to get six months to study whatever he wanted.

Most predicted it would have something to do with bird sounds. In 1929 a Hollywood movie studio had called Doc to see if Cornell could provide background birdsong for a film. Doc had no library of recordings to offer, but he had been so fascinated by the possibility of recording for the movies that he had invited the film-makers to Cornell to try to record some birds. In those early days of talking movies, the only way to record sounds was by filming them on "motion picture sound film" with "sound recording cameras." You actually played the sound back on a screen. That spring a Hollywood crew drove to Ithaca in a truck bulging with thirty thousand dollars' worth of recording equipment. They picked Doc up at the Cornell campus and rumbled straight to a city park to see if they could record birds that were singing there.

The men staggered around the park beneath heavy cameras and microphones, usually scaring the birds away before they could get near. But they did manage some film, and when they ran it back at McGraw, they could faintly make out the scratchy voices of a Song Sparrow, a House Wren, and a Rose-breasted Grosbeak. Doc heard the future in those sounds.

For the next few years, Doc and an ever-growing group of students kept experimenting with ways to record birdsong. At the center of the action was Albert Brand, a pudgy stockbroker from New York City who had quit his Wall Street job to study birds at Cornell. Brand used his wealth to buy recording machines that he, Doc, and three engineers tinkered with day and night. They cranked up the volume as loud as they could to make the faint bird voices come out. A professor whose office was next to the laboratory where the experiments were being carried out described hearing "the wildest of yells, roars, crashes and shrieks as dials are turned and films projected. Lowered in pitch and augmented in volume, the recording of a yellow warbler's cheery little voice sounds for all the world like coal roaring down a chute into somebody's cellar."

Within two years, Brand and fellow Cornell student Peter Keane had recorded forty bird species. It was Brand who finally came up with the winning idea for Doc's sabbatical leave: why not tour the country, recording the voices and filming the

THE SOUND MIRROR

One afternoon, Cornell ornithology student Peter Keane, in New York City on a break, wandered over to the construction site of Radio City Music Hall. He found it interesting that giant parabolic reflectors were being installed as part of the sound system. These huge, dish-shaped devices were used to concentrate and amplify sound, and to screen out unwanted noises.

Keane asked himself if the reflectors might not work on a smaller scale. What if you built smaller, portable reflectors that you could carry by hand to a bird's nest? The Cornell physics department just happened to have in its attic a mold that had been used to build parabolic reflectors during World War I to detect enemy planes. Keane and his fellow student Albert Brand used it to build a big, shiny dish they called a "sound mirror."

One morning they carried it out into a field, set it on a tripod, suspended a microphone in the middle of the dish, and aimed it at a singing bird. It worked. Most of the usual background noise, such as barking dogs and rushing rivers, was gone—and the birdsong was loud and clear.

behavior of America's rarest birds? Then Americans could hear their songs and see them move *before* they became extinct. A Cornell team could install the new sound equipment in a truck like the one from Hollywood. Brand himself would raise the money. They would work in the spring, when birds would be singing loudly to attract mates and defend their breeding territories.

Doc loved the plan. He had long regretted that people could no longer hear the Passenger Pigeon's coo, the toot of the Heath Hen, the Labrador Duck's quack, or the Great Auk's grunt. These were sounds Americans had once known well. Now, because these birds were extinct, their songs had passed forever from human memory. Other birds were in danger of slipping away, too. Brand's idea could preserve their voices before they were lost. And if they succeeded, Cornell would be known as a world leader in sound.

Of course, there was another reason for Doc's enthusiasm. He had never forgotten the two Ivory-billed Woodpeckers he and Edna had seen in Florida back in 1924, the birds that had been shot soon after. There had been no more confirmed sightings of Ivory-bills since. But suddenly there was hope again. Doc had learned that in 1932 a lawyer named Mason D. Spencer had found and shot an Ivory-bill in a Louisiana swamp. Ornithologists had rushed to the scene and found several more Ivory-bills nearby. Recording the birds on film would give Doc a second chance, a different way to "collect" these beautiful phantoms without killing them. Doc wanted to study their life cycle and to see if somehow the species could be preserved in its natural setting before it was too late.

Allen told reporters that the "Brand–Cornell University–American Museum of Natural History Ornithological Expedition" would be a new kind of "hunting" expedition whose members would "leave guns at home and would 'shoot' the birds with cameras, microphones, and binoculars."

The idea caught the imagination of both the public and the scientific world. According to one newspaper article, "Never before in the world's history has any expedition started afield with so highly sensitive equipment." Cornell was flooded with applications from scientists, curators, and bird-watchers who wanted to go along.

While Brand raised funds and Cornell professor Peter Paul Kellogg installed the recording machines in a truck, Doc recruited the team he wanted: Doc himself would film and photograph the birds, Brand would pay the bills and help work on sound, and Kellogg would operate the equipment at the truck, while George Sutton, a sharp-eyed bird artist, would help identify birds and scout for sites.

But Doc needed one more person. It had to be someone who knew birds and who possessed the strength and agility to do the heavy work of the project, someone who could climb trees like a monkey. Whoever it was would have to be cheerful enough to take orders from cranky professors at five in the morning. This person would have to be able to fit in with everyone, for surely the team would meet people around the United States whose views and ways clashed with theirs.

In the end, it wasn't a hard decision at all. As Doc put it in the press release that went to newspapers, "James Tanner, graduate student, was invited to accompany the expedition as handy man to act in any necessary capacity."

Jim Tanner
operates Cornell's
newly designed
sound reflector, or
"sound mirror,"
hoping to hear an
Ivory-bill

CHAPTER SEVEN
SHOOTING WITH A MIKE

With the expansion of vision beyond the gunsight, an entire new world unfolded like the
opening of a bud of a most wonderful, beautiful flower.

—Dr. Boonsong Lekagul, ornithologist from Thailand

United States — 1935

THE CORNELL TEAM, MINUS BRAND, WHO WAS IN ILL HEALTH, ROLLED OUT OF ITHACA in two freshly polished black trucks on February 13, 1935. The smaller truck was stuffed with machines for recording sound. The bigger vehicle contained camping gear and photographic equipment, food, tents, and other supplies. Folded down into a wooden box on top of the bigger truck was an observation platform that could be cranked up like a giant jack-in-the-box to raise a photographer to bird's-nest level, twenty-four feet above the ground.

The team drove to Florida, where it searched without luck for Ivory-bills. But the members didn't waste their time. Each morning they practiced recording, faithfully rising before dawn so that Florida's milk trucks and tractors, roosters and barking dogs wouldn't drown out the birds. They worked out a routine: after arriving at a field or swamp, Paul Kellogg would drag a stool around in front of the sound truck, clamp earphones to his head, and begin twisting the dials that adjusted sound levels. Meanwhile, Jim Tanner would hoist the sound mirror in front of him like a jouster with his shield and advance steadily on the birds, dragging his boots slowly through the prickly brown Florida scrubland. As Tanner approached with the great gleaming disk, the birds would turn to face him, puffing up their feathers and singing loud songs of warning, all of which would be recorded by Kellogg at the sound truck.

In April, after a month in Florida and Georgia, the trucks passed over the wide, brown Mississippi River at Natchez, Mississippi, and pulled into Tallulah, Louisiana, a flat, dusty crossroads whose office buildings and houses were bunched around a town square with a courthouse in the middle. The team drove the trucks a few blocks past the square and got out in front of the law office of Mason D. Spencer, the man who had found and shot an Ivory-billed Woodpecker just three years earlier.

Spencer was a heavyset, red-faced politician who dressed in a white linen suit and wore a straw hat. He rolled his own cigarettes, exhaling clouds of blue smoke that clung to the ceiling of his cluttered office. After introductions, Spencer gathered the Cornell scholars around a table and unrolled a map. Pointing to the spot where he had shot the bird, he repeated the epic tale of his famous discovery. It all started during a meeting of Louisiana wildlife officials in New Orleans, when someone passed on a rumor that an Ivory-billed Woodpecker had been seen in the Singer Refuge near Tallulah, along the Tensas River. After the laughter died down, someone else cracked that the local moonshine must be pretty good up there if anyone believed that.

But Mason Spencer wasn't laughing. He had a hunting camp on the Tensas, and everyone knew it. They were goading him, waiting to see how he would react. "I've seen them myself," he declared. The others challenged Spencer to prove it by shooting one and bringing it back to New Orleans. Spencer said he'd be delighted to, if they'd write him out a state permit. Spencer got his permit, shot his bird, and, in April of 1932, went back to New Orleans and tossed a freshly killed male Ivory-bill on a conservation official's desk.

After a respectful silence, Professor George Sutton worked up the nerve to say what was on the minds of Tanner, Allen, and Kellogg as well. Clearing his throat, he said, "Mr. Spencer, you're sure the bird you're telling us about isn't the big *Pileated* Woodpecker?" The room fell silent as Spencer glared at Sutton. "Man alive!" he snorted. "These birds I'm tellin' you all about is *kints*! . . . I've known kints all my life. My pappy showed 'em to me when I was just a kid. I see 'em every fall when I go deer huntin' . . . They're *big* birds, I tell you, big and black-and-white; and they fly through the woods like Pintail Ducks!"

That was good enough for the Cornell team, especially the part about the Pintail Ducks. That was exactly how Ivory-bills flew, and only someone who had seen them could know it. Spencer sketched out a map to a guide's cabin in the swamp, and the team got back in the trucks. Before long they were splashing through a flooded land, craning their heads out the windows to gawk up at giant trees that rose like cathedral walls from both sides of the road.

After a few miles they were waved to a halt by a man driving an empty farm wagon behind a team of mules. He introduced himself simply as Ike, and said he'd

Ike's wagon makes its way into the vast swamp

been sent to help them. They gladly pulled the trucks to the roadside, transferred their gear into his wagon, and climbed aboard. The mules plunged into the trees, following a watery trail for five miles to the cabin of J. J. Kuhn, a local warden who had agreed to help them search for Ivory-bills. It was too late in the day to start out, so they unrolled their sleeping bags on his big screened-in porch and stacked their gear in the kitchen. They were glad to hear Ike's son, Albert, already chopping wood for the fire that would cook their dinner.

"DID YOU SEE IT?"

The next morning, Doc, Tanner, and Sutton filed out behind Kuhn into the great swamp forest. Kellogg stayed behind to work on the sound truck. A rainy March had turned the woods into an enormous puddle, and now only the highest ground was above water. Kuhn led the way with a long, swinging stride. Even in the muggy heat he wore a long-sleeved flannel shirt buttoned to the neck and a hunter's cap to protect his head. He rarely spoke. The always chatty Professor Sutton splashed behind in a crisply pressed shirt and a well-knotted tie. Young Tanner also dressed neatly and usually kept his thoughts to himself. Doc, always rumpled, brought up the rear.

Soon all the men's trousers—both rumpled and crisply pressed—were plastered to their legs. But, although soggy and uncomfortable, the men were enchanted by the vine-tangled wilderness they were passing through. The forest was fragrant with blossoms and spring warblers were singing. Best of all, it was still two weeks before mosquito season. They slipped along a narrow trail, then waded into a wide lake that Kuhn called John's Bayou. Finally, Kuhn stopped before a towering oak whose bark appeared to have been peeled like a giant carrot. Long strips of dead wood dangled in loose sheets from the trunk; they must have been pried back by something very powerful. Everyone looked around for suspects, but there were none in sight.

For two more days the men sloshed through the bayous. The forest was alive with hammering woodpeckers, but they heard no Ivory-bills, not even a call or a rap. By the third day Kuhn had grown anxious. He kept insisting that the birds were there, that he had seen them himself just weeks before. Finally, he decided the only choice was to head into deeper water. The team doubled back through John's Bayou and, soaked to the skin now, turned due east, wading into what Sutton described as "a twilight of gigantic trees, poison ivy, and invisible pools."

The four explorers spread out and advanced in a straight line like beaters on an African safari, shouting frequently since they couldn't see each other. After they had gone a few hundred yards, Sutton thought he heard Kuhn yelling excitedly, but he couldn't make out what he was saying. Sutton took off in pursuit, calling back over his shoulder for Tanner to follow, and Tanner began sprinting as he shouted back to Allen. When they all caught up with Kuhn, his face was red with excitement. "Right *there*, men," he said as he jabbed his finger into the forest. "Didn't any of you *hear* it?" They cupped their hands to their ears. All they could hear was Pileated Woodpeckers.

So they advanced again, this time more slowly and closer together. Kuhn and Sutton were the first to hop onto a huge cypress log, teetering along it with their arms out so they could see and hear more clearly. Suddenly Kuhn stopped and whispered, "There it goes, Doc! Did you see it?" He grabbed Sutton's shoulder and whirled him around, nearly sending them both toppling off the log. Kuhn was shouting now. "A nest! See it! There it is, right up there!" Sutton was uncertain. He *had* seen something, an arrow-like shadow of some kind, fly to a dead tree, but he wasn't sure what it was. Gradually his eyes began to focus on a big oval hole high up in that same tree.

Kuhn, overjoyed, grabbed the distinguished Ivy League professor and led him in a jig as Tanner arrived in a rush, nearly knocking them both off the log. Then Doc Allen entered the picture, crashing through the woods like a bear. The four of them, laughing, danced on the log, mostly to honor Kuhn, since they still hadn't seen what he had. And then, as they were dancing, a bird began to call. They froze in place. "The cry was strange, bleatlike," Sutton wrote. "The moment I heard the sound I knew I had never heard it before."

At that moment a large black-and-white spear went streaking toward the tree. Crouching low, Tanner and Sutton finally got their first look at the legendary bird, and Allen beheld an old friend again at last. A female Ivory-bill flew into the nest, poked her head out, and flew away again. "Much white showed in her wings," Sutton remembered. "Her long black crest curled jauntily upward at the tip. Her eyes were white and fiercely bright. Her flight was swift and direct."

An Ivory-bill, like the one seen by Allen, Sutton, and Tanner, flies away from its nest

Then she returned with her mate. The male was a little bigger, with a backward-sweeping red crest instead of a forward black one. The male caught sight of the men and turned his head to look at them directly. He flew to a limb overhead and looked down with head cocked, through first one brilliant amber eye and then the other. "What a splendid creature he was!" wrote Sutton. "He called loudly, preened himself, shook out his plumage, rapped defiantly, then hitched down the trunk to look at me more closely. As I beheld his scarlet crest and white shoulder straps I felt that I had never seen a more strikingly handsome bird."

So there it was. After years of rumors, dead ends, and false alarms, Doc had his second chance and the Cornell team had its star bird for the sound project. Not just a single bird, either, but a mated pair with a nest. That night, back at Kuhn's cabin, they turned their attention to the next task. They had found the Ivory-bill; now the job was to record its voice. But how in the world would they ever haul 1,500 pounds of America's most sensitive sound equipment into the spongy middle of nowhere?

THE NIGHTMARE SWAMP

The wilderness in which the Cornell team now found themselves was a patch of the Mississippi River's delta, a vast area formed when the great river, swollen from melting snow and rains from as far north as Minnesota, flooded its banks each spring, carrying with it a load of riverbottom soil known as silt. Thousands of years of floods had spread the silt like a rich layer of brown frosting over an area five hundred miles long and fifty miles wide. Mississippi delta silt was some of the best soil in the world for growing trees. The bottomland forest, as it was called, was prime Ivory-bill country.

Most of the delta had been cleared and settled, but there was one great wilderness forest southwest of Tallulah still standing. The Tensas River, an old, slow-moving channel of the Mississippi, snaked lazily back and forth through its trees as it had long before human memory. In the 1830s a few pioneers had arrived to clear away trees and plant cotton along the river's banks. After a levee was built to hold the Mississippi's spring floods, more families came, building grand white-columned houses. Set apart from the big houses were clusters of crude shacks, quarters for Negro slaves who soon outnumbered whites nine to one along the river.

Behind the buildings were fields of cotton which, after the cotton bolls burst open, shone bleached white in the blazing sun. And just behind the cotton fields, always in sight, loomed the imposing trees of the nightmarish Tensas swamp. People believed that everything that crawled, howled, lurked, snapped, hooted, screamed, and slithered lived right back there, just beyond the fields. And they were right. After visiting the swamp in 1907, Theodore Roosevelt wrote, "We saw alligators and garfish; and monstrous snapping turtles, fearsome brutes as heavy as a man with huge horny beaks that with a single snap could take off a man's hand or foot . . . Thick-bodied water moccasins, foul and dangerous, kept near the water, and farther back in the swamp we found and killed rattlesnakes and copperheads."

THE TAENSA

The Tensas swamp is laced with huge mounds that, from the air, look like welts in the muddy earth. They are burial mounds of the Taensa Indians, the group that occupied the area before whites appeared. When the French explorer Sieur René-Robert Cavelier de La Salle traveled down the Mississippi to explore the delta in 1682, he visited a Taensa village and was welcomed warmly. The French described the Taensa as a people who lived in large, well-made buildings. They worshipped the sun and kept a fire burning all the time in a temple that had a roof decorated with the carved likenesses of three birds. When a chief died, they sacrificed a number of his friends and relatives so that they could accompany him into the afterlife. Later, most of the Taensa Indian population was killed by smallpox and measles viruses carried by whites, against which the Indians had no defenses.

In 1861 the Civil War broke out, and the following year Yankee troops seized control of much of the Mississippi River. Yankee soldiers descended upon the Tensas plantations, stealing horses, cattle, and food, freeing slaves, and terrorizing those remaining in the plantation homes, most of whom were women and children.

Planter families faced a desperate choice: they could either stay at home and wait for the Yankees or flee to Texas through the dreaded swamp. Many said their prayers, set fire to their cotton crops, and plunged on foot and horseback into the dark trees.

Seventy years later, in 1935, when the Cornell ornithologists hunted for Ivory-billed Woodpeckers in this same swamp, there was little evidence of the cotton society or the Civil War. The ruins of a few plantation buildings lay smothered beneath fragrant flowering vines. Trees had sprouted back so quickly along the Tensas that they soon blended in with the giants behind them. It was as if no one had ever lived there.

But the rest of the vast Mississippi delta had changed plenty. Railroads finally reached the Tensas River sometime around 1900, ushering in lumber crews and logging equipment. For about thirty years loggers had been steadily closing in on the Tensas swamp from the north and the south, like a giant set of alligator jaws. Soon it was the last big scrap left of the Mississippi River bottomland forest, once a green carpet that had stretched from Memphis, Tennessee, to the Gulf of Mexico.

The giant oaks and ashes and sweet gums along the Tensas seemed doomed, too, until, one day in 1913, the dry scratch of a pen against paper in New York City froze the powerful jaws of development in midbite. On March 28 of that year, Douglas Alexander, a portly white-haired man in a business suit, stood beside his elegant wife, Helen, in a New York City courthouse and looked on as she signed her name to a deed that gave the Ivory-bill one last chance. She signed it not to help woodpeckers, but so that her husband's company could sell sewing ma-

---

TR, BEARS, AND IVORY-BILLS

In the fall of 1907, President Theodore Roosevelt set out to kill a bear "after the fashion of the old Southern planters." That meant tracking it on horseback and using dogs to sniff it out. TR's huge hunting party chose the Tensas River swamp, notoriously thick with bears.

The President thought he had seen big trees before, but he nearly got a cramp in his neck gawking up at the skyscrapers growing from the bottom of the swamp. "In stature, in towering majesty, they are unsurpassed by any trees of our eastern forests; lordlier kings of the green-leaved world are not to be found until we reach the sequoias and redwoods of the Sierras."

The wild creatures were just as amazing. TR saw minks, raccoons, possums, deer, black squirrels, wood rats, panther tracks, and, of course, bears, one of which he killed. But one creature impressed him above all. "The most notable birds and those which most interested me were the great Ivory-billed woodpeckers. Of these I saw three, all of them in groves of giant cypress; their brilliant white bills contrasted finely with the black of their general plumage. They were noisy but wary, and they seemed to me to set off the wildness of the swamp as much as any of the beasts of the chase."

chines. For Douglas Alexander was president of the Singer Manufacturing Company, and Singer needed oak trees. Many Singer machines folded down into cabinets, becoming flat-topped tables when no one was sewing. Women around the world loved the oak cabinets because they were beautiful, and because they saved space in cramped tenements and crowded rooms. But America was running out of oak trees.

Alexander's scouts had found one last forest of uncut hardwoods. It was for sale in the Mississippi delta, in northeastern Louisiana. Singer bought the Tensas swamp for about nineteen dollars an acre and immediately declared its new property a "refuge," meaning that the trees were not to be cut without the Singer company's approval. Hunting was forbidden. The forest began to appear on Louisiana maps as the Singer Refuge and was later called by conservationists the Singer Tract.

But Singer soon found that it was much easier to get the word "refuge" put on a map than to keep hunters out of a game paradise. Families had been shooting their food in these woods for years, and powerful politicians like Mason Spencer often retreated to hunting cabins along the Tensas River where damp bottomlands teemed with bear, deer, and turkey. No one was going to quit hunting on account of a sewing-machine company.

Finally, in 1920, the Singer company offered Louisiana's Fish and Game Department the chance to manage Singer's land as long as the state agreed to hire wardens to regulate hunters and tree poachers. J. J. Kuhn was employed as a Singer warden when Tanner, Allen, Kellogg, and Sutton showed up in Tallulah. At first he had seen his job simply as keeping hunters out. But for the past three years, ever since Mason Spencer had shot the big woodpecker, he had found himself guiding scientists through the forest looking for Ivory-bills. His curiosity about the great birds had grown by leaps and bounds, to the point where he not only knew where the birds were, but knew the entire forest by heart. What had seemed simply a game forest was now something more. Kuhn had come to realize that his place of work was a sort of forested oasis, an intact natural island surrounded by a rising tide of lawns, paved roads, and cotton fields.

THE BIG RED S

In 1913, the year that the Singer Manufacturing Company bought a big chunk of the Tensas swamp, the company sold 2.5 million machines around the world to countries as far-flung as Spain, Russia, or Japan. Singer's headquarters, the Singer Building, was the tallest building in the world, rising forty-seven stories above Broadway in New York City. As president of the Singer company, Douglas Alexander commanded one of the biggest business empires in the world. He was fabulously rich, and so admired that in a few years he would even be knighted.

Paul Kellogg squints at Ivory-bills through
a spotting scope while Jim Tanner listens
to their sounds through recording
equipment sheltered beneath the tent

CHAPTER EIGHT
CAMP EPHILUS

When Nature has work to be done, she creates a genius to do it.

—Ralph Waldo Emerson

Singer Refuge, Louisiana—1935

LATE INTO THE NIGHT AT KUHN'S CABIN, THE CORNELL RESEARCHERS WENT OVER their options for transporting the sound equipment five miles through the muck to the Ivory-bills' nest. The choices all looked bad. Driving the trucks through the swamp would be impossible. The sound truck alone weighed nearly a ton, and the ground was like soup.

Finally they hit on an ingenious plan. They would drive the trucks to some dry place in Tallulah and take the sound truck apart, disconnecting the instruments from the truck. Then they would rebuild the recording system in Ike's farm wagon and turn *it* into the sound truck. Ike's mules could pull it into the swamp. They'd build a camp on some dry spot near the Ivory-bills' nest, and from there they could spend as much time as they needed to film, record, and study the birds. It just might work.

They drove their trucks into town, and Doc went to ask the mayor for a work site. He gave them a choice location. A few minutes later, puzzled prisoners at the town jail peered out through the bars of their cell windows at two heavy black trucks pulling up onto the lawn. Then three well-dressed strangers got out, greeted them pleasantly, and began to jerk wires from the inside of one truck, placing them neatly on the ground. When word got around about what they were doing, one of the prisoners hollered out, "Hey! I know right where the peckerwoods are if you can get me out of here!"

By the dawn of Monday, April 8, all the instruments were rebuilt in Ike's farm wagon, and the four mules clopped off for the swamp. Having finished his sketches of Ivory-bills, Professor Sutton had departed for Texas to scout out other rare birds, leaving Allen, Kellogg, and Tanner to observe the woodpeckers. It took all day to reach the nest, with Kellogg and Allen riding the two lead mules and Tanner, Kuhn, and Ike's son, Albert, scrambling behind on foot. They finally stopped in front of a giant oak tree about three hundred feet from the Ivory-bills' nest.

The Cornell team transports its sound equipment to Camp Ephilus

The men flung a wide canvas tent, like a circus big top, over the sound truck, and then propped it up with small saplings, lashing the canvas to nearby trees. They stacked up palmetto fans between the roots of a tree and spread their sleeping blankets on top, hoping the pile would be high enough off the ground to keep them dry at night. Mounting a pair of binoculars on a tripod, they aimed it at the nest hole and scooted a lawn chair behind it so that one of them could sit and watch the nest during daylight. Then they pointed the sound mirror toward the nest hole and built a cooking site. They called their new home "Camp Ephilus," a pun on the Ivory-bill's genus name, *Campephilus*.

Doc Allen takes his turn at the spotting scope

The next afternoon both Ivory-bills briefly left the nest. Jim Tanner scrambled up an elm that stood just twenty feet from the nest tree and hammered a plank between two limbs. He quickly added to it a small frame over which he draped a scrap of canvas. He backed down the tree again, nailing boards into the trunk as he descended. Now they had a "blind" that would give them a closer look if the birds would accept such near neighbors.

The men settled down to the nuts and bolts of an ornithologist's work. They worked in shifts, never taking their eyes off the nest hole during daylight, recording in their journal even the most ordinary behavior of the birds. As Doc's notes from April 11 show, the Ivory-bills eyed their new neighbors nervously:

[8:45 a.m.] Tanner went up to the blind and pulled up the camera. The female once flew to the nest hole but became alarmed and flew away after climbing to the top of the stub. While Tanner was setting his camera, the male came and entered the nest. [I] frightened the male from the nest by rubbing the tree. In about twenty minutes it returned, climbed to the hole, looked around and looked in, but after about half a minute or more it became alarmed by the rattle of the camera and flew off. Ten or fifteen minutes later it returned and . . . finally entered the hole.

Doc, Tanner, and Kellogg knew they were taking a risk. If they scared the birds off, there was no assurance there were any more to be seen. Even worse, the disturbance could disrupt the birds' breeding season. On the other hand, saving the species from extinction depended on knowing enough about it to make recommendations. This was the best chance anyone would probably ever have. Their expedition had become more than a sound-recording experiment; now they were on a rescue mission as well.

The Ivory-bills' pattern was the same every day: the male and female took turns

The male Ivory-bill arrives at the nest hole as the female appears at the opening. The Cornell team took this close-up from a blind built in a nearby tree

incubating—sitting on—the eggs inside the nest hole. The male took the night shift, staying with the eggs until about 6:30 a.m. At that hour he rapped on the inside of the hole, delivering an impatient message that echoed through the forest. If his mate was late in arriving, he stuck his head out of the hole and uttered a few "yaps" or "kents," but he never left his post until she got back. When she did, the two birds seemed to chatter for a while, and then the male remained at the nest for about twenty more minutes, preening his feathers, before zooming off somewhere, probably to find food or to sleep. For the rest of the day, the couple took turns incubating in shifts of about two hours. The female always left at about 4:30 in the afternoon, and stayed away all night.

Another forest creature who slept little and took off at night was Jim Tanner. Now he knew what Doc had meant by describing him as the team's "handy man" who would "act in any necessary capacity." At Camp Ephilus, Tanner was the cook, the builder, the climber, the porter, and the acrobat who was able to get the camera and the sound mirror closest to the birds. He could soon operate all the equipment. Since there was only room for two to sleep at the camp, every night Tanner sloshed two miles to Ike's home, crawled into bed with Albert, and fell into a brief, deep sleep. He was up at 4:30 each morning and back in camp, hauling water through the darkness and chopping wood to get a fire going and cook for his professors. After scrubbing pots, he took up his morning watch of the Ivory-bills, which usually began at about 6 a.m. Far from feeling used, he was thrilled. What did sleep matter when you had the chance to study North America's rarest bird close-up? Dirty, sticky, bug-bitten, always a little tired, and still not yet twenty-one, Jim Tanner figured he was one of the luckiest people on earth.

THE SPRINT WEST

After five days of observing the birds, the team came to a crossroads. Though they longed to stay with the Ivory-bill family until the eggs hatched and the young were raised, they had other rare birds to record, birds scattered throughout the whole country. Kuhn hiked in with a telegram for Doc, a reminder from a colleague that if they didn't get to western Oklahoma by May 1, they would lose their chance to record another of America's rarest birds, the Lesser Prairie Chicken.

Once again a late-night talk produced a plan. If all went as they hoped, they could dash to Oklahoma, record the prairie chickens, and make it back to Camp Ephilus in two weeks. By then, the young Ivory-bills should have hatched and still be in the nest, not quite ready to fly and still being fed by their parents. J. J. Kuhn volunteered to check in on the nest while they were gone. That seemed the best they could do.

Doc sent for Ike and the mules, the sound truck was reassembled, and the team rumbled west—straight into the worst dust storm in U.S. history. Sunday, April 14, 1935, began as a day with a piercingly blue sky, but when the wind started blowing, it swept up the soil of Oklahoma and Kansas into a terrifying black wall of dust seven thousand feet high. The dust blew eastward all the way across the country, even dumping prairie soil onto ships in the Atlantic Ocean. Reports of the mighty storm kept the Cornell team stalled for three days in western Louisiana. When they began to drive again, they saw a landscape that seemed as strange as the moon's. With the windshield wiper going all the time, they coughed their way across the prairie.

ECOLOGICAL DISASTER

During World War I, prairie farmers plowed under their deep-rooted native grasses and planted shallow-rooted wheat in their place to feed troops overseas.

Prosperity followed until, for some reason, it simply stopped raining. By the time the Cornell team got to Oklahoma, there hadn't been a soaking rainstorm for four years. But the wind blew unceasingly, whipping the unbound, powdery soil into towering clouds of dust that blotted out the sun, covered machinery, and suffocated farm animals. People slept with masks on, tried to keep the dust out of their food, and prayed constantly.

You can hear the wind's bleak howl in the background of their recordings of the Lesser Prairie Chicken, finally accomplished on the eighth day. With Camp Ephilus and the family of Ivory-bills always on their minds, they drove almost nonstop to Colorado and Kansas, making more recordings, and then raced back to Louisiana. There was no way to telephone Kuhn. They only hoped they weren't too late.

CRAWLING SAWDUST

Little things rule the world. —Harvard biologist Edward O. Wilson

The team didn't make it back to the Ivory-bill nest until May 9, nearly a month after they had left. They had missed their chance; the birds were gone. Kuhn had visited the nest late in April and found the pair behaving strangely. Each bird spent most of its time nervously poking its head into the nest hole, then entering the nest for just a few minutes, and then flying off to another nearby tree. They preened themselves almost constantly, and after a while they stopped bringing food to the nest altogether. Then they disappeared.

The scientists examined the nest thoroughly, hoping for clues that would tell them why the birds left without rearing young. Inside the hole were tiny fragments of eggshell and a thin, even layer of what looked like sawdust. There was no sign of blood or struggle, no torn feathers or other evidence that a hawk or an owl or a raccoon had slipped into the nest and carried off or eaten the young. They swept the nest contents into a paper bag and took it back to their hotel in Tallulah. The next morning, Doc emptied the contents of the bag onto a desk and turned on a lamp for a closer look. Tanner and Kellogg gathered around. The "sawdust" quickly sprang to life under the hot lightbulb. Soon the desk was seething with tiny mites that stormed up their hands, biting all the way. Yelping, the three men raced for water, scrubbed their arms, and bagged up as many of the tiny creatures as they could. Doc sealed them in an envelope and mailed them off to Cornell so that a mite expert could tell them what species they were.

There turned out to be nine different species. Some ate only wood, fungi, and algae, but at least three ravenously ate warm-blooded creatures. Allen remembered how nervous the adult Ivory-bills had seemed at the nest, and how much time they had spent preening their feathers. He wondered if the newly hatched birds hadn't been overwhelmed by this army of mites, or if maybe they hadn't even been born at all. Maybe the adults had been so busy trying to pick mites out of their feathers that they hadn't spent enough time incubating the eggs. But then again, the egg fragments probably meant the young had hatched. So what had happened to the chicks?

The next day, Allen, Kuhn, Tanner, and a visitor from the National Park Service scouted on horseback for another nest. After seven tough miles they heard faint sounds similar to the calls the parents had made when exchanging shifts at the nest back at Camp Ephilus. Kuhn dismounted and tiptoed closer until he spotted a male's red crest disappearing into a hole nearly fifty feet up in a dead oak hanging over a small clearing. The men tied up their horses and concealed themselves in a thicket of poison ivy and catbrier for two hours, watching the nest and scribbling notes. Around noon they saw the sign they were looking for—the male flew into the nest with a "big borer grub held lengthwise in his bill"—baby food. And sure enough, a few minutes later they heard what Doc described as "a weak buzzing from the young . . . Apparently they were too small to swallow the grub for [the male] left [and flew] with it to a tree one hundred feet away and apparently swallowed it himself."

At last they had what they wanted: a nest with young birds inside to observe. They hustled back to Tallulah, reassembled Ike's wagon for sound at the jail, and dragged everything back into the swamp, arriving at the new nest before noon on May 14. But once again the forest was still and the Ivory-bills were gone. They waited all afternoon for the birds to return, then gave up and examined the nest. Again there was no sign of blood or struggle. There were no eggs or shells or feathers. This time there weren't even mites. It was as if the parents had cleaned the nest carefully and checked out.

Doc Allen kept trying to fit the clues together into a pattern, but every time there were missing pieces. In some ways the birds' behavior at the two nests was similar to that of birds at a third nest Kuhn told him he had observed two years earlier. These woodpeckers had also seemed to be working hard to incubate eggs and feed young, except that they were extremely nervous and jumpy. Sometimes they changed places twenty times an hour. They finally deserted the nest before their nestlings could fly or feed themselves. Kuhn had peered into the nest, but it had been empty. He didn't think mites had been there. To Doc, the one link between the three nests was that in each case the adults had managed to hatch their young, but then lost them soon after.

Allen thought about predators. Ivory-bill nests had big holes, big enough for a Great Horned Owl or a large hawk to enter, but there was never a sign of a fight or a killing. What was going on? He began to wonder if something very serious might be happening here. Was the problem genetic? Maybe there were just too few birds left to produce sturdy stock. Maybe all the years of logging and specimen hunting had finally left so few adults so closely related to one another that the offspring they produced could stay alive for only a few days. It was

GIVING VOICE TO BIRDS AT LAST

The Cornell sound expeditionaries—mainly Tanner, Allen, and Kellogg—traveled almost fifteen thousand miles and came home with ten miles of sound film.

They recorded the voices of nearly one hundred of America's rarest birds, including this Golden Eagle, and later transferred them to phonograph records that found their way into thousands of homes.

Besides the only voice recording ever of the Ivory-billed Woodpecker, they recorded the honk of the Trumpeter Swan—then almost as rare—the gobbling Lesser Prairie Chicken, screaming hawks, and the eerie wail of the Limpkin. The Cornell pioneers gave more feathered creatures a place in the choir and made ours a more tuneful America.

what happened in many species when first cousins mated. Family groups of Ivory-bills had grown increasingly isolated, and interacted only with each other. There were only a very few mates to choose from. Scientists call this "inbreeding."

Doc Allen hoped there was still time to save the species. He felt that extinction was not only a tragedy but a sign of human defeat, and that he had a moral responsibility not to give up on a fellow creature if it could be saved. But he needed to know more. Just as a doctor needs to understand the behavior of a virus or a bacterium in order to prescribe a cure for an infection, he had to know exactly why these birds were dying in order to save them.

The Cornell crew headed west again to record other birds, and then back to Ithaca loaded down with steel canisters of sound film. The most prized segment of all, the part that got shown again and again all over the country, lasts only thirty seconds. It begins with a big Hollywood director–like voice (Kellogg's) saying, "Ivory-billed Woodpecker; Cornell Catalogue—cut one." Then the viewer sees Ike's truck being hauled into the Tensas swamp by four mules moving away from the camera, with Tanner and Albert scrambling behind on foot.

Then the magic part: suddenly there's footage of a male Ivory-billed Woodpecker poking his head into and out of a nest, close-up and alive with frantic energy. He gives off a series of loud, hornlike "yaps" and "kents." The sounds continue as the camera moves to Doc, sitting in the lawn chair at Camp Ephilus, shirt buttoned up against the

Cornell's historic film captures the Ivory-bill at its nest

bugs, looking through the binoculars at the nest as a campfire crackles in the background. Finally the camera swings to Paul Kellogg twisting dials in the sound truck, and then the screen goes black.

Three-quarters of a century later, those brief tooting sounds remain the only recordings ever made of the Ivory-billed Woodpecker's voice, and the film the only record of what the astonishing bird looked like as it moved. The members of the Cornell sound team almost certainly returned from their adventures proud to have made a major contribution to science, and to have documented images and sounds important to American history. But as they settled down to their lectures and classrooms and labs, they must have had trouble keeping their minds from straying to the giant mystery they had left behind at the Singer Refuge.

Jim Tanner's 1931
Model A Ford
coupe

CHAPTER NINE
WANTED: AMERICA'S RAREST BIRD

Saw old sign[s of woodpeckers], lots of almost impenetrable vines, and no Ivorybills.

—A common entry in James Tanner's journal

Riverbottom Swamps of the Southeastern United States—1937–1939

JOHN BAKER WAS A MAN WHO KNEW HOW TO GET WHAT HE WANTED. HE HAD NEVER backed down as a fighter pilot in World War I, and afterward, as an investment banker, he had developed a well-earned reputation as a hard negotiator. But this tough man loved birds, so when he was offered the chance to direct the Audubon Society in 1934, he walked away from banking without even a glance back at Wall Street. He immediately recruited an all-star team of young scientists, bird experts, and teachers, including Roger Tory Peterson, the remarkable young artist and educator whose new *Field Guide to the Birds* was creating thousands of new bird-watchers overnight. Baker set out to broaden the Audubon Society's mission so that it conserved not only birds, but also water, soil, plants, and other wildlife—whole ecosystems. As Baker put it, "Every plant and animal has its role to play in the community of living things. There is no such thing as a harmful species; all are beneficial."

When Baker found out that a few Ivory-billed Woodpeckers were by some miracle still alive in Louisiana, he made up his mind to save the species. It was one thing to let a creature slip away without knowing it, but the Cornell films and recordings proved there was still hope. Like Doc Allen, Baker was convinced that the key to the

Ivory-bill's survival was knowing more about it. He quickly raised thousands of dollars for an "Audubon Research Fellowship" that would fund an expert to spend three years studying the Ivory-bill under Doc Allen's supervision at Cornell. Among other things, this expert would try to locate every Ivory-billed Woodpecker left in the United States. After carefully studying the bird's biology, health, and history, the expert would write an action plan for saving the species—like a doctor writing a prescription for a feathered patient. It would be the most detailed conservation plan ever attempted in the United States for a single bird species.

At Cornell, once again Doc knew exactly who he wanted. But this time Jim Tanner's commitment to the Ivory-bill would have to go much deeper. Always on the move, he would have to track the bird through wild haunts like a sheriff pursuing a fugitive. For years he would have no permanent address.

Doc explained the hardships to Tanner. A normal life with friends and family would be impossible. He would usually be beyond the reach of telephone or telegram, and he would have to solve his own problems. Three years was a long time. It could get lonely.

But to Jim Tanner, all this weighed less than a feather compared to the rewards of such a chance. He could learn so much of what he hungered to understand. He could contribute to the science of ornithology. His work would count toward a doctoral degree, and then maybe help him establish a teaching career. Best of all, maybe he could help save a magnificent bird that he had grown to love. He was twenty-three and unmarried, and he even had a car: a 1931 Model A Ford coupe that was as tough as a small truck. Tanner didn't even hesitate: Doc had his expert.

At Cornell, Doc and Tanner carefully developed the goals of the investigation:

1. Tanner would try to find out where Ivory-bills had lived historically—all the places they had ever been found. That meant a huge amount of reading, writing to experts, visiting libraries and museums, talking to old-timers with long memories, and listing and mapping every report ever written down by anyone who had collected an Ivory-bill specimen.

2. He would also try to discover where Ivory-bills lived now. He would visit every

major swamp and cypress forest from North Carolina to Texas if he had to. He would interview hunters and foresters, game wardens and bird-watchers, and try to find every Ivory-bill still alive. He would make a list and a map showing where they were. By comparing the current map to the historical map, he could show how much of their habitat had been lost and what their favorite types of forest had been.

3. He would study the ecology of the species—the relationship between the Ivory-bill and its environment. What did it eat? How did it find its food? Did anything eat it? Mites? Mosquitoes? Owls? If it couldn't find its favorite food, what else would it eat, if anything? Did it need certain kinds of trees for food and shelter?

4. He would investigate the bird's reproductive and nesting habits. What kinds of trees will an Ivory-bill nest in? How high off the ground are the nests? How many eggs does it lay? If one clutch of eggs fails, will it produce another in the same year? If so, how many times? How much food does a nesting family need, and how much space is needed to provide it? Do both parents always incubate eggs and feed young? And, of course, he would try to answer the question that so plagued Doc—why were the nests failing to produce surviving young at the Singer Tract?

5. Finally, Tanner would create a plan to protect the Ivory-billed Woodpecker. This would be a detailed blueprint that conservationists could use.

Tanner prepared carefully for his new life. He bought dozens of one-cent postcards to send to Doc, Baker, and his friends and family while he was on the road. He figured out how to unbolt the front seat from his car, lift it out, and turn it into a bed that could be laid on the ground. That would save time and money, and would let him sleep in the woods if he needed to. He packed maps, tools, books, binoculars, boots, a first-aid kit, clothing, and camping gear. He made address lists of Doc's con-

ECOLOGY

In the 1930s and 1940s, ornithologists became more and more interested in ecology—studying a bird's whole natural environment and how it interacted with everything around it—not just in the biology of an individual species. James Tanner was an ideal candidate to study the Ivory-bill because his interests were very broad; he knew that in order to learn how to save the Ivory-bill, he had to know how the whole forest worked.

Those who study natural ecosystems learn that humans simplify and nature complicates. For example, a tree plantation has fewer species of plants and animals living in it than the forest it replaced. The original forest had more ecological "niches"—the small environments in which species evolve ways to find food, protect their young, and stay safe from predators. A big, ragged forest ecosystem like the Singer forest had thousands of niches, many more than the farms and settlements in the surrounding cleared areas.

tacts and carefully tucked away the letter of introduction Doc wrote for him to show to strangers. It read:

> To whom it may concern: You will find Mr. Tanner extremely reliable and trustworthy, and if you prefer that your information should get no further than him, I know that he can keep a secret when it concerns the welfare of the Ivory-bill. —Arthur A. Allen

Tanner found drawings of a Pileated and an Ivory-billed Woodpecker shown side by side. A printer shrank the page to pocket size and ran off dozens of copies for him. These cards would be valuable, since the two species were so often confused. They would also give him something to leave with the many people he would interview—it was half business card, half wanted poster.

He celebrated the holidays with his parents in Cortland and on January 4, 1937, took off in his roadster, passing through the low hills he had hiked as a boy, over the Catskills, down to New York City, and on toward the South. His car had no radio and he wasn't much of a singer; his dreams were his entertainment. He was off to do what no one had ever done, and it happened to be the thing he wanted to do most. He would do his best to find all remaining Ivory-bills, to understand them, and to help them. As he motored toward the great southern river swamps, he could have titled his journey "Wanted: America's Rarest Bird."

IVORY-BILL ALIASES

James Tanner made this list of the names that the Ivory-bill was called in scientific literature or by people he met:

Pearly Bill
Pearl Bill
Log-god
Log-cock
Woodcock
King Woodchuck
King of the Woodpeckers
Indian Hen
Southern Giant Woodpecker
Pate or Pait
Ivory-billed Caip
Tit-ka (Seminole name)
Grand Pic Noir a bec blanc
Poule de bois [in southern Louisiana]
Grand pique-bois [in southern Louisiana]
Habenspecht
Elfenbeinschnabel-Specht
Kent [northern Louisiana]

THE ADAPTABLE RESEARCHER

On January 20, 1937, Jim Tanner followed a hand-sketched map to a dirt road which led to a landing along the Altamaha River in southern Georgia. The Ford pitched to a stop around noon. Tanner got out and stretched. The day was fine and warm. An old-timer was fishing from a crude wooden rowboat just offshore, and they fell into pleasant conversation. A few minutes and four dollars later, the boat was Jim Tanner's. Tanner piled in the gear he needed, pulled the car off the road, and shoved off downstream.

He had come to the Altamaha River to check out an Ivory-bill record that was now eleven years old. Somewhere in his research he had seen a report that in 1926 a man named Verster Brown Sr. had spotted an Ivory-bill in a swamp on the river near Baxley, Georgia. The details of his sighting were good enough to make it seem worth exploring. Tanner stayed on the river for the next five days, paddling fifty miles in all. Often he would raise the oars out of the water and cock his ear for the Ivory-bill's cry. He never heard it. Most of the trees along the river had been recently cut, and there wasn't much wildlife of any kind to be seen or heard. Local people had little useful information. Finally he dragged the boat up to the shore and hitchhiked back to his car. "It did not produce results," he wrote in his journal, "but it was a grand trip on a pretty river."

He drove south to Florida, the state with more records of Ivory-bill sightings than any other. Pulling the drawing of two woodpeckers from his shirt pocket, he introduced himself to dozens of loggers, hunters, trappers, poachers, and wildlife managers. They gave him still more names of old-timers who knew the land. He dutifully looked most of them up. But everywhere the story was the same—yes, Ivory-bills, or Log-cocks, or Lord God birds, had been here, but not for a while. The rumors were thick as mosquitoes, and like mosquitoes, rumors seemed to breed more rumors.

Early in February, Tanner reached the Everglades. Sun-burned game wardens with leathery faces squinted at him, stroked their chins, and said yes, they thought perhaps they had seen the birds among the cypress trees maybe fifteen or

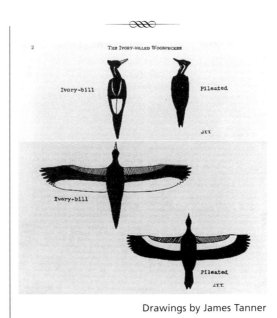

Drawings by James Tanner

IVORY-BILLS VERSUS PILEATEDS

Tanner believed that most people who told him about Ivory-bills were really reporting the much more common Pileated Woodpecker. Both birds are very big and both have black-and-white coloring. Males of both species have red crests, adding to the confusion.

Tanner wrote, "The position of the white on the wing is by far the most reliable field character at all times," he wrote. "In the Ivory-bill the white is on the rear half of the wing and is visible on the back when the bird is perched and its wings folded. In the Pile-ated the white is on the front half of the wing and is hidden when the wings are folded."

twenty years ago. One guide, Dewey Brown, said he had heard Ivory-bills recently from Big Cypress Swamp. He was happy to show Tanner the spot, but said it would take a few days to get there. By now, Tanner was learning to size up exactly how much of his time any particular rumor was worth. This one was promising, but not that promising. "I told him I would return next year with more time for a decent trip," Tanner noted.

Tanner's final Florida destination was the Suwannee River, a spot famous for Ivory-bills. William Brewster and Frank Chapman had floated down this river in 1890, killing one Ivory-bill and hearing another. Two years later, Arthur Wayne and his "crackers" had shot Ivory-bills for Brewster and others. Now, more than forty years later, a few of the men who had collected for Wayne were still alive. They were wrinkled old woodsmen with long memories. As Tanner later wrote, they said that "after Wayne's work there Ivory-bills were very unusual and that he had secured almost all of them." Looking around at the grand trees lining the banks, Tanner hoped it wasn't true. He thought the Suwannee still looked good enough to investigate.

Tanner's map showed a landing, a few miles downstream from Old Town, where the road went down to the riverbank. Maybe he could find another boat or canoe there. For the next hour, Tanner guided the Ford on a jolting, head-bumping ride along two beaten ruts that finally ended at a deserted clearing by the river's edge.

Tanner got out as the dust settled around him. With darkness fast approaching, he walked into the trees and loaded his arms full of twigs and limbs, then stacked them into a tidy pyramid and lit a fire. Minutes later he was contentedly crouched over his supper when he heard a truck rattling down the road. It came to a stop, and several men spilled out. Waving a hasty greeting, they hurried off to gather firewood. After a while Tanner heard bootsteps approaching his fire. Three faces appeared out of the dark, lit by the blaze. The men squatted on their heels and introduced themselves. They said they were there for some night fishing.

Many men in Tanner's situation would have been frightened out of their wits. He was unarmed and surrounded by strangers in the middle of nowhere. Maybe they were after his car. Maybe his money. But Jim Tanner was, as Doc Allen liked to put it, "adaptable." He could fit in anywhere.

"What are you doing here?" one of the men began. Stirring his fire, Tanner answered, "I am looking for peckerwoods." The men were silent. He then launched into his well-rehearsed speech about how there were two kinds of big woodpeckers in these parts, one common and the other rare, and that he was trying to find the rare one. As he was speaking, Tanner could see their eyes narrowing with suspicion. Tanner rambled on until one of the men suddenly burst out laughing. The others soon followed.

When he could finally speak, the first man said, "By golly, I thought for a minute you really *were* hunting for a peckerwood!" Catching his breath, he explained to Tanner that in those parts "peckerwood" could mean either a bird or a woodsman. Years before, another stranger had come down to the river looking for the human kind. With revenge in his eyes, he was after someone who had crossed him and had escaped on the river. The men had assumed Tanner was after the same fugitive until they realized he actually was looking for a bird.

The strangers tromped off into the blackness to set out their fishing lines, and then banked their own fire to a roaring blaze against the cool night. They yelled over for Tanner to join their party, and he did. "We had a big meal of fried fish, baked yams, and biscuits. I ate my share even though I had already had one supper. Then they loaded their truck and near midnight disappeared up the narrow road." It was one of many days and nights that didn't turn out the way Tanner planned, but it showed that just about anything could, and would, happen on an expedition like this.

HARD TRAVELING

For the next three weeks Tanner drove, hiked, galloped, and waded around Florida chasing leads, scribbling notes, leaving his pictures behind, and trying not to get frustrated. The Suwannee had a promising habitat, but no Ivory-bills. The best lead yet took him to a forest near Brooksville, Florida, where an Ivory-bill had been reported only the year before. Tanner searched the area with two local men and at last found a sign: "a dead pine from which the bark had been completely scaled, apparently the work of an Ivory-bill." Tanner assumed the bird was only passing through, though, since the habitat didn't seem good enough for nesting birds.

On March 17 he took off west for Louisiana and the Singer Refuge, the one place where he knew he could actually find Ivory-bills. Two items of good news awaited him: J. J. Kuhn, the woodsman who had guided the Cornell sound team so expertly before, was available and eager to help. Just as happily, Tanner and Kuhn could use the Singer Manufacturing Company's cabin in the woods as a base of operations. That meant they could stay in the woods all the time except when they had to go into town for supplies.

Tanner and Kuhn concentrated their search on the east side of the Tensas River. On March 26 they finally spotted a pair of adult Ivory-bills winging swiftly through the flooded backwater called John's Bayou, and after four days of hard searching Tanner found their nest, chiseled in the top of a sweet gum. All day long the parents took turns shuttling long white grubs to a single open-mouthed baby, who constantly yapped for food.

J. J. Kuhn, warden of the Singer Refuge and Tanner's indispensable companion

The very next day, the little bird hopped up onto the lip of the nest hole, steadied itself, spread its wings, and leaped into its first flight. It never returned to the nest again, and the family's address shifted to a tree about a quarter mile away where they slept—or "roosted"—together each night.

"[The young bird] flew well from the start," Tanner wrote proudly. "The family hunted together close to the nest tree for the next two months. The youngster grew stronger and more independent every day. Within a month it could join its parents on food-finding trips two miles away from their home tree. By mid-July it was nearly as big as its mother and father, a powerful flyer and a mighty hunter of grubs." It still called to be fed, though, as young birds often do. Tanner found himself delighted by the prowess of this young bird, but worried that the family had produced only one egg. "This pair of birds gave no indication of nesting a second time," he wrote, "even though they nested so very early."

Throughout May and June, Tanner and Kuhn combed the forest for more Ivory-bills. The daily hikes installed a mental map of the forest in Tanner's head. He came to know where the waterways called bayous emptied into the forest, where the lakes were, and how the forest trees changed when the ground got lower or higher, wetter or drier. The Ivory-bills nested and slept in sweet-gum and oak trees that sprouted from dry ridges that had long ago been banked up by the Mississippi's floods. Tanner called them "first bottoms."

Kuhn and Tanner usually split up so that they could cover twice as much ground. They searched mainly in the morning, when the birds were most active. Tanner's strategy was to stop walking and listen about every quarter mile, since the Ivory-bill's call carried about half a mile. He always heard Ivory-bills before he saw them. When he wasn't searching for birds, he was working on other parts of his research project, doing things like counting trees, collecting and inspecting grubs, scouting new locations, and investigating the biology and ecology of the Ivory-bill in countless other ways.

Sometimes he just sat still. As a young boy, he had practiced sitting still outdoors for long periods of time. Now this was helping him in his profession. As he sat and listened, swatting bugs, taking notes, trying not to scratch his poison ivy welts, daydreaming and dozing every now and then, he occasionally tried to imitate the Ivory-bill's call to see if the birds would answer. They never did. Once he tooted through the mouthpiece of a saxophone. No luck. But from time to time an Ivory-bill would call on its own from somewhere way off in the forest, sending him springing to his feet and tearing off after it, through the underbrush.

During the winter and spring of 1937, Tanner and Kuhn found evidence of adult Ivory-billed Woodpeckers in seven different parts of the Singer Tract. Since adult Ivory-bills mated for life and stayed together all year round, Tanner assumed there were seven different nesting pairs, even though he saw only one young bird the whole time. Another parent was seen winging across a lake with a grub dangling from its bill, which almost certainly meant there was a young bird to be fed, but they couldn't find the nest and never saw a nestling.

Tanner kept wondering why all those adults produced so few young birds. Was Doc right about inbreeding? Were they tormented by mites? Or was it something else they hadn't even thought of? After the small Ivory-bill family Kuhn and Tanner found on March 26 had abandoned its nest tree, Tanner shinnied high up the sweet gum and inspected the nest. Once again there was no evidence of parasites or mites, nor were there signs of struggle. The disappearing Ivory-bills were still a mystery.

When summer came, broad leaves made treetops almost impossible to see and the air filled with swarming mosquitoes. Tanner rolled up his bedroll, packed his boots, and got ready to hike out to Tallulah and head home. But just before he left, he and Kuhn heard news that hit them both hard: the Singer company had sold six thousand acres of its land to a lumber company, and logging had already started. The land was on the west side of the Tensas—not the best Ivory-bill habitat in the forest, but now the lumbermen had their feet in the door. Even worse, Singer had sold the rest of the west side to the much bigger Chicago Mill and Lumber Company—which had a major sawmill in Tallulah. Singer was even allowing an oil company to drill test wells in prime Ivory-bill habitat.

Tanner said goodbye to Kuhn on June 29 and spent another month tracking leads in Louisiana and South Carolina before he turned north toward home. Back at Cornell, he sorted through the hundreds of pages of notes he had compiled, and began to reflect on what he had learned so far.

In his first season of sleuthing, he had been able to find Ivory-bills only at the Singer Tract. There was still promising habitat at Big Cypress Swamp and the lower Suwannee River, both in Florida. These sites merited follow-up visits. Four other places looked good, too, but less so. The birds at Singer were not reproducing well, and he still didn't know why. But he now knew more about the kinds of trees the birds liked, what they ate, and how much space a nesting family seemed to need.

Casting a shadow over everything was the sale of Ivory-bill habitat at Singer. Tanner didn't let his emotions show easily, but there was desperation in his year-end report to John Baker of the Audubon Society. Time was running out. "Those woods should be *preserved*," he wrote. "That area should be a national monument, and I strongly recommend that a movement be started towards that goal, even though the lumbering interests and possibility of oil present difficulties."

Looking back at that winter and spring, Tanner knew there were still many more questions than answers, but one thing was certain: he had done some hard traveling. He wrote a tribute to his indestructible Ford that might well have reminded him of himself. "It has been the first car to break a way over many a muddy road," he said. "It has had several springs broken, mufflers knocked off and running-boards knocked loose, bumpers broken on trees, and the front axle bent. But it still runs."

The Singer Tract was the last significant
scrap of a vast riverbottom forest that
once covered millions of acres

CHAPTER TEN
THE LAST IVORY-BILL FOREST

The Ivory-bill has frequently been described as a dweller in dark and gloomy swamps, has been associated with muck and murk, has been called a melancholy bird, but it is not that at all . . . The Ivory-bill is a dweller of the tree tops and sunshine; it lives in the sun . . . in surroundings as bright as its own plumage. It is true that the man trying to watch and follow these birds is probably in the shade and mud, among the fallen trees and running vines, but that does not affect the Ivory-bill in the least. He stays above all that, and is a handsome, vigorous, graceful bird.

—James Tanner

1937

By now the Ivory-bill was to be found only in one place: the Singer Tract in northeastern Louisiana

Singer Tract, Louisiana—December 1937–October 1938

FOUR MONTHS LATER, TANNER WAS BACK IN THE SOUTH. HIS RESEARCH OF THE PREVI-ous spring had narrowed down the number of likely habitats for Ivory-bills, and there was no time to waste. The place he wanted to explore most was a swamp around the Santee River in South Carolina. Museum specimens and local reports left no doubt that many Ivory-bills had once lived there. Local experts confidently predicted that eight to twelve nesting pairs still remained.

Early in December, Tanner and a guide pulled on their boots and set out to comb every part of the Santee swamp for Ivory-bills. Eleven days later they came back disappointed. While they had seen a few stripped trees, Tanner wasn't sure Ivory-bills had done the work. And they hadn't heard a single call.

The Santee search made Tanner rethink how much habitat Ivory-bills really needed. "I believe [the local experts] have underestimated the range of the birds, and so overestimated the numbers," he wrote. In short, he feared that there wasn't nearly enough food for eight to twelve pairs in a forest the size of the Santee's. He thought

THE CAROLINA PARAKEET

Southern U.S. forests once teemed with emerald-green parakeets sporting a bold yellow streak where the wing met the body and a blood-red patch around the eye. Audubon said they were so abundant that they covered orchards "like a brilliant coloured carpet." Now the species is extinct. Why? Farmers killed them because they ate fruit. Market hunters shot, stuffed, and sold them to collectors. Hatmakers loved the green plumes, and hunters found the birds easy targets. When one bird lay dead on the ground, others in a flock often joined it, making themselves targets, too. The last Carolina Parakeet, Inca, died in the Cincinnati Zoo in 1918.

back to the Ivory-bill family he had studied in the spring at the Singer Tract. They were nomads. Within a month, even the little bird had been able to fly two miles from its home tree in search of food. He realized that it must take a lot of territory to contain enough food for a family of Ivory-bills. The Santee was less than half the size of the Singer Tract. Tanner figured it was big enough for only two, maybe three, pairs at most.

With this ominous new theory, Tanner gunned the engine of his Ford and swung toward Louisiana, racing through the Georgia hills and across the Mississippi to Tallulah in a single day. By dusk Tanner and J. J. Kuhn were walking single file along the slippery trail to their cabin, balancing sacks of groceries on their shoulders as they picked their way around mudholes and stepped over logs.

Beginning at dawn the next day, Tanner explored the Singer Tract day and night. Step by step he learned where the bayous ran and how the forest changed from its flat soggy bottom, laced with vines, to its drier ridges. He came to sense the subtle changes of the seasons—the lengthening of shadows, the fragrance of blossoming vines, the smell of wet leaves, and the steady electric hum of insects. Finally these patterns converged into a picture of the whole magnificent forest.

Tanner's visits to other swamps in the South had usually been disappointing because loggers had sliced the forests up into small patches. Less than halfway through his study, he began to suspect that the Singer Tract was the last big uncut swamp forest left in the entire Mississippi delta—maybe in the whole South. The Singer Tract was the one forest that looked and felt and smelled and sounded as it must have thousands of years before. There was a good chance that every single species that had ever lived in this forest was still there except for the Carolina Parakeet and the Passenger Pigeon—both extinct. Everything else—from Ivory-bills, panthers, and wolves to grubs, mites, and frogs—was still there.

Feather-topped cypress trees fringed the lakes inside the Singer Tract

Tanner was beginning to realize that in order to understand the Ivory-bill's life history, and to save it at the Singer Tract, he had to know the forest completely, to understand it as a single colossal organism throbbing with life. So the whole forest became Tanner's lab, and it fascinated him as much as any species within it, even the Ivory-bill. Often he began hiking before the sun rose and was still out after dark.

Winter was by far Tanner's favorite season. Ivory-bill calls carried a long distance through the leafless forest, and he could spot the birds more easily when they flew through the bare limbs. Plus, there were no mosquitoes or snakes. One winter morning he made his way to an Ivory-bill roost tree while it was still dark, hours before the woodpeckers would be active. Plumping up a cushion of palmetto fronds, he settled himself against a tree to hear the forest wake up. It was great entertainment, he thought, and he didn't even need a ticket.

Just as the first pink stripe appeared behind the black-silhouetted trees, Barred Owls signed off the night shift with their final *"Who cooks for you, who cooks for you-all"* hoots. The spreading sunlight brought the day crew to life, singer by singer and song by song.

THE RED WOLF

A Red Wolf can be any color from tan to black. Smaller than its cousin the Gray Wolf, it once hunted deer and smaller mammals in forests, marshes, and swamps from Pennsylvania to Texas and in southeastern states. Many were shot and trapped early in the twentieth century as suspected killers of cows and sheep. At the same time, their habitat was cleared and drained.

By the late 1930s, only two populations remained in the United States, including some at the Singer Tract. In 1967, the Red Wolf was declared endangered. Six years later, with the species nearing extinction, biologists captured 14 wolves so they could breed in safe, zoo-like situations. Now there are 270 to 300 Red Wolves, of which 50 to 80 live in the wild.

Brown Thrashers led off the dawn chorus with a hoarse, once-repeated *churr* that welled up from the brambles. White-throated Sparrows chimed in next, with a high melody whose first four notes sounded like "Here comes the bride." Then the amazing Winter Wrens burst onto center stage, stub-tailed midgets who threw back their heads and belted out the longest song of any bird, rattling their entire frames with the effort. By the time the late-sleeping Ivory-bills finally appeared at their hole to preen their feathers, the forest was bathed in light. By then, Tanner noted, seven other woodpecker species had already called.

Sometimes surprise guests appeared during his silent vigils. One December morning Tanner was seated on the ground, listening for Ivory-bills, when the vines in front of him rustled and the stiff palmetto fronds gave way to something big and solid. At first the glossy black back that passed slowly before his eyes seemed to belong to a small horse. Then, suddenly, he realized it was a wolf walking along a log. When it plopped silently to the ground and vanished into a thicket, Tanner raised himself to a half crouch so he could see better. The wolf came out of the brush and passed slowly across a clearing maybe thirty steps away. "He was handsome, powerful . . . with a deep chest and a lean belly, self confident, alert . . . black from tip to tail," Tanner wrote. Cupping his hands, Tanner tried to squeak like a wounded bird to catch the wolf's attention, but it trotted off.

The forest became silent and still at midday, when creatures active in daylight hours seem to take a break. The forest pulse quickened again at dusk and stayed brisk until sundown, which ushered in a whole new cast of characters. One night Tanner rowed a small wooden boat out into the middle of a lake, put his oars at rest, and remained silent as he scanned the moonlit water. "The forest stretched away for miles from the black wall of trees surrounding the lake," he later wrote. "The air shook with noise . . . The chorus of frogs came from all sides . . . loudest by weight of numbers were the tiny cricket frogs on the floating duckweed . . . sitting and beating out their rasping notes." He flicked on a flashlight. The beam swept across the surface of the water until it caught "a glowing coal that burnt for a moment and then went out—the eye of an alligator that sank beneath the surface."

Day or night, poisonous snakes were a huge worry, especially around Greenlea Bend. Timber Rattlesnakes slithered out from their winter dens just as spring covered up the foot trails with vines, leaves, and brambles. The "thick-bodied water moccasins" and Copperheads that Theodore Roosevelt had seen on his hunting trip were still there, too, and plenty of them. Since Tanner and Kuhn couldn't look up for birds and down for snakes at the same time, there were many unscheduled meetings. Once, as Kuhn went charging through a thicket of vines after a bird, his boot came down on a rattler. The unmistakable sound sent him leaping in the only direction he could—straight up. Then, penned in by brambles on all sides, he landed on the only place he could—straight down. The snake was still there, rattling away. Heart pounding, Kuhn jumped again, with the same result, and kept on jumping until the snake darted away.

In spring and summer, the two men wore long-sleeved shirts with all the buttons closed tight to the neck and the collars turned up, and sometimes they wore their hats jammed down over their ears. But still the insects bit and stung them. Annoying as it was, it gave them something in common with all the other warm-blooded creatures of the forest, and they had no choice but to accept it.

The most awesome event in the woods occurred when one of the giant trees fell. This usually happened after a hard rain, when a grand old monarch's soaked crown became so heavy that the trunk could not hold it up any longer. Then, as Tanner wrote, "the quiet of the woods would suddenly be broken by a resounding crack . . . then a series of loud snaps merging into a roaring crescendo as the tree crashes downwards to hit the earth with a dull, echoing boom. The echoes quickly die away, but the forest still seems to hold its breath until gradually the birds resume their song, the normal quiet sounds return, and the listener collects his scattered thoughts."

In the evenings, Kuhn and Tanner ate their supper together by a kerosene lamp on the cabin's screened-in porch. Since they often split up during the day, they used the night to catch up. "We talked . . . just as Mark Twain's river pilots endlessly discussed the details of the river's course," wrote Tanner. "Although learning of the Ivory-bill and its life history was our goal, the forest was our working place and we had to know it—[how] to find our way, to travel quickly and to know where to hunt."

The two men's deepening friendship was rooted in a respect for the forest. Jim Tanner and J. J. Kuhn were after something different from the game pursued by the hunters who had passed through the forest before them. Unarmed, and with their minds and hearts wide open, they were hunting for knowledge.

SONNY BOY

As Christmas of 1937 approached, Tanner and Kuhn set out to count all the Ivory-bills in the Singer Tract. It was too early in the season for nests, but the birds were easy to see and hear in the leafless forest.

Quickly they found three pairs and another female who had no mate. That made seven birds—a good start. But for some reason they couldn't find the young bird they had seen the spring before. Then, on December 22, rain began to fall, drumming steadily on their cabin roof for more than a week. The water collected in puddles in front of the cabin; then the puddles gathered into ponds. When the ponds merged into a sheet of water that made hiking impossible, Tanner drove back to New York for the holidays.

It was mid-February before he could return, and now there was no time to lose. Nesting season lasted from January to May, so there might already be young birds in the forest. Early on February 17 Tanner discovered a pair of Ivory-bills nesting in a live red maple tree at John's Bayou, not far from where he had observed the small family the year before. He built a blind and settled in to observe. More than anything, he wanted to know how many baby birds there were, but it might take weeks before nestlings were strong enough to appear at the hole. With the whole forest to cover, he didn't have that much time. He took a chance. On the morning of February 24, when both parents had flown away, Tanner hastily drove a ladder of spikes up toward the nest hole. He was about halfway to the nest when the adults flew back and caught him red-handed.

They dug their claws into a nearby tree and glared back over their shoulders at the huge invader. Then the male flew to the nest tree and hitched down the trunk toward Tanner, backing him down the spikes until he hopped onto the ground and stepped away. The male flew off but soon returned with a grub in its bill, disappearing into the nest. Tanner let out a sigh of relief, for early writers such as Audubon had reported that Ivory-billed Woodpeckers were easily spooked and would desert their nests for even the slightest of reasons.

Later the parents flew off again and Tanner scurried back up his ladder, completing it as he climbed. When he got to the hole, he reached his hand inside and felt around. It was surprisingly warm. Something made "a long, scraping buzz." Probing gingerly around the entire nest, Tanner's fingers came to rest upon the soft feathers of a single little bird. There was nothing else inside at all, not even pieces of eggshells. As he scrambled down the ladder in time to beat the parents, Tanner's mind blazed with the same question that had plagued him ever since the Cornell sound expedition three years before. Once again, only one nestling—*why?*

Ten days later, the baby bird appeared at the opening, poking its head out curiously for the first time. It was clearly a male. Soon he would be strong enough to fly and leave home. Tanner decided to try to "band" him with a lightweight collar around one foot so that researchers would be able to identify him anywhere he went and track his movements.

On March 6, banding day, Tanner and Kuhn waited at the nest tree for the adults to take their usual morning break. When they did, Tanner raced up the spike ladder. But as he drew near, the young bird poked his head out of the opening, spread his wings, and flung himself into the air. Tanner reached out instinctively and caught him. The bird struggled and squawked, but Tanner managed to fasten the band around one leg and gently place the young bird back in the cavity. However, their acquaintance was far from over. As Tanner lingered by the hole to whittle away a small branch that had blocked his view of the entrance, the young bird appeared again and took a second leap, this time plunging down past Tanner's grasp.

The bird fluttered into a tangle of vines, where he lay yelping and squawking. Tanner scrambled down the ladder and pulled him out of the thicket. He was, Tanner

---

BANDING BIRDS

John James Audubon was the first person to "band" a bird. In 1803 he tied silver threads to the feet of Eastern Phoebes in Pennsylvania—birds that migrate south in the winter. The next year, some of them returned to the same place to nest.

German scientists banded gulls and other birds that flew over the Baltic Sea in 1903. People who found these birds in France had no idea what the bands meant. They thought maybe the bands had been attached by sailors aboard a sinking ship.

Today the U.S. Fish and Wildlife Service issues people permits to fasten lightweight bands to the legs of birds. Each band is colored and has a specific number. The data tell us about the birds' migration routes and traveling speed, and how old they are. Jim Tanner is the only person ever known to have banded an Ivory-billed Woodpecker.

Sonny Boy meets
J. J. Kuhn

wrote, "yelling loud enough to be heard in Tallulah." Gently handing the bird to
Kuhn, Tanner fumbled for his camera and started snapping pictures before the parents got back. He had already wasted six shots before he realized he hadn't focused
the camera. He jammed more film in the camera and was firing away again when he
realized he hadn't even opened the lens. He had rarely been this flustered in his life.
He took a deep breath and made himself slowly go over how to operate a camera.

By this time, the young Ivory-bill had taken over the situation. No longer wailing, he
climbed out of Kuhn's cupped hands and hopped sideways onto his wrist, perching on it
as if it were a limb. Then he hitched his way up along Kuhn's arm and perched on his
shoulder as Tanner snapped photos. Seeking the safety of a high perch, the bird continued up Kuhn's collar, scaled his head, and hopped atop his cap, puffing up his feathers to
make himself look bigger. When Kuhn reached for the bird with his hand, the bird
pecked at it, puncturing the skin. Tanner later wrote, "Though only a nestling, it had the
imposing and elegant appearance of the Ivorybill and the quick and confident actions."

When Tanner ran out of film, he wrapped the bird loosely in two soft handker-
chiefs, buttoned him inside his shirt, and climbed back up the tree, placing him gently
in the nest. This time the young bird stayed inside. As Kuhn and Tanner watched in
hiding, the mother returned. To their relief, she fed her son without hesitation. The

father flew in a bit later with his own billful of grubs. "Sonny Boy," as Tanner and Kuhn called the little bird, became history's only known banded Ivory-billed Wood-pecker, and the only young Ivory-bill ever captured close-up on film.

THE FATAL FLAW

Seventeen months later, in October of 1939, Jim Tanner straightened his tie, cleared his throat, and faced the members and staff of the National Association of Audubon Societies in New York City. It was the third and final year he would deliver a report about his Audubon Research Fellowship on the Ivory-billed Woodpecker, and this time he illustrated his presentation with a slide show. The first slide showed his beloved car—as trusty a companion as any cowboy's horse.

Tanner showed slides of Kuhn, of "Sonny Boy," of adult Ivory-bills, of towering trees and moonlit lakes, and then he got down to his conclusions. He estimated that there might still be about twenty-five Ivory-billed Woodpeckers left on earth, scat-tered throughout four or five large areas in Florida, Louisiana, and South Carolina—though he had seen the birds only in the Singer Tract in Louisiana.

He reported fewer and fewer Ivory-bills every year at the Singer forest. The numbers were as follows:

1934—seven pairs that gave birth to four birds
1935—no data
1936—six pairs and six young birds
1937—five pairs and one unmated adult, producing two young birds
1938—two pairs and three unmated adults; three young birds
1939—one pair and three unmated adults; one young bird

He didn't think there was enough evidence to blame the decline on inbreeding. In fact, it seemed encouraging that he had been able to find at least one successful nest in each of the three years of his study—that meant the species was still able to reproduce.

No, there was a much more serious problem, getting bigger each day. The birds were starving to death. The Chicago Mill and Lumber Company's giant band saw in Tallulah was devouring the last nesting, roosting, and food trees of the Lord God bird as fast as logs could be fed in. Time was running out fast for the Ivory-bill.

Tanner had finally identified the Ivory-bill's fatal flaw, at least at the Singer Tract. These birds needed a forest home big enough so that somewhere a few old trees were always dying natural deaths at any given time. These could be trees that were injured by lightning or wind or weakened by disease or old age, but they had to be still standing as they died. Only in such trees did the beetle larvae called grubs bore into still-tight bark to lay their eggs. Those grubs were almost the only thing that Ivory-billed Woodpeckers ate.

Why didn't these birds just change their diet and eat other things? What possible advantage was there to being such finicky eaters? Some birds, like Mourning Doves, draw nourishment from hundreds of plant species, and others eat many kinds of insects, as well as other prey. Tanner's theory was this: there were so many big, fat grubs under the bark of a tree just after it died that the Ivory-bills had formed a habit of looking for those trees and very little else. Large birds like Ivory-bills need a lot of food, especially when they are raising a young family, and the banquet under the bark could feed the Ivory-bills' families for a long time. Of all the woodpeckers, only the

Ivory-bill was strong enough to pry off bark while it was still bound tightly to the tree. Others had to wait until the tree became weaker and the bark looser. In other words, the Ivory-bill had its own private stash of grubs that no other woodpecker could reach.

But once logging started at the Singer Tract and the food began to run out, the birds couldn't change their habits fast enough to look for other kinds of food. The problem was that there were only so many newly dying trees in a forest at any one time. The forest had to be very big to contain enough Ivory-bill food. The Ivory-bills could cover great distances to find the trees—and mates traveled together—but the trees had to exist somewhere.

According to Tanner's calculations, a mated pair of Ivory-bills needed to live in an uncut or nearly uncut forest of six square miles in size to furnish enough grubs to feed a small

GRUBS

With nearly 300,000 species, beetles are the most common insects on earth. They live everywhere except the oceans. Beetles pass through four life stages to adulthood—egg, larva, pupa, and adult. The second, or larval, stage is called a grub. Ivory-billed Woodpeckers gobbled grubs from three beetle families, Cerymbycidae, Scolytidae, and Buprestidae, all of which developed from eggs laid under the bark of dying trees. There was a lot of nutrition in these white, flat-headed grubs, some of which grew to three inches long and an inch thick. But the Ivory-bills had to get them fast, for they molted into pupa within just a few weeks.

family. That was 36 times more room than Pileated Woodpeckers needed, and 126 times more than Red-headed Woodpeckers did. No wonder the Ivory-bill was in desperate straits: the Singer Tract was the last scrap left of the huge carpet of trees that had once covered the entire Mississippi delta, and now it was disappearing by the minute. Tanner told his audience, now raptly attentive, that day by day there was "less dead wood, fewer insect borers, and less food for woodpeckers." "This decrease in food supply," he said, "has been the only thing I have found which could seriously affect the numbers of Ivory-bills."

Tanner presented a plan to meet the needs of both woodpeckers and loggers. His map divided the Singer Tract into three types of areas:

1. "Reserve" areas—the best Ivory-bill places, like John's Bayou, not to be cut at all;

2. "Partial cutting" areas—not the best part of the forest for Ivory-bills, but places they still sometimes used; and

3. Logging areas—places not used much by Ivory-bills, where logging could take place.

Unfortunately, the Ivory-bill's favorite food trees—sweet gum and Nuttall's oak—were also the species that made Chicago Mill the most money. Tanner recommended that loggers spare all such trees whose tops were already dead or dying, since the wood was inferior and birds could use them for roosting, nesting, and perching. For the same reason, he urged that dead trees of all species be left standing. He even came up with an idea for *increasing* woodpecker food in the forest—by "girdling," or choking, some trees so they could die standing up, instead of cutting them down. That way the grubs would infest them and the woodpeckers would have food. He recommended that no more railroad tracks be laid in the forest, that hunting be banned, and that few people be allowed to visit until the Ivory-bill could recover. He urged that most logging be done in summer and fall rather than winter and spring, when Ivory-bills nested.

Tanner stood before his audience as the world's most knowledgeable expert on America's rarest bird. He finished his presentation by appealing to the Audubon Society with all the force that three years and forty-five thousand miles of intense study could deliver. They had before them both an emergency and an opportunity. "I believe that I have seen almost every bit of virgin timber in the South," he said, "and unreservedly, the Singer tract has the finest stand of virgin swamp forest . . . [it] should be preserved, as an example of that forest with all its birds and mammals—a true bit of the North American wilderness."

He had done what he could. Now the ball was in Audubon's court.

All across the
South, trees that
took centuries to
grow, like these
cypress trees in
Perry, Florida, were
leveled in hours by
men with their
new machines

CHAPTER ELEVEN
THE RACE TO SAVE THE LORD GOD BIRD

All the men in the village worked in the mill or for it. It had been there seven years and in seven years more it would destroy all the timber within its reach. Then some of the machinery and most of the men who ran it and existed because of and for it would be loaded onto freight cars and moved away.

—William Faulkner, *Light in August* (1932)

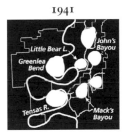

1941

The Singer Tract, with the Tensas River snaking through it. Important Ivory-bill habitats are in white

Northern Louisiana—1941-1943

THE CHICAGO MILL AND LUMBER COMPANY MADE WOODEN BOXES—CASKETS, SHELL boxes, wagon seats; anything with four sides, a top, and a bottom that a customer might order. After the Great Chicago Fire of 1871, it soon needed more wood than the pine forests around the Great Lakes could supply. In 1898 it bought a sawmill in Greenville, Mississippi, that came with a warehouse full of logging equipment and twenty-five thousand acres of big delta trees. Hiring dozens of local men, it set about planing the best wood into boards for furniture makers and slicing up the second-class wood into box parts. Soon Chicago Mill's tugboats were proudly pushing its lumber to market down the Mississippi River on the company's private fleet of barges, often escorted by its private steamboat, the *Hazel Rice*.

In 1928 Chicago Mill bought another sawmill in the shadow of a huge wilderness forest owned by none other than the Singer Manufacturing Company. There were mammoth trees in those woods, oaks and sweet gums that would send furniture makers down on their knees in praise. Chicago Mill built a box factory in Tallulah, Louisiana, and went to see the Singer people.

The timing was perfect. High in his New York City skyscraper office, Singer president Douglas Alexander had taken to fuming at "flappers," blaming them for a sudden drop-off in U.S. sewing machine sales. He didn't care if they bobbed their hair and smoked and danced and drove—but couldn't they just keep *sewing*? To Alexander, emancipated women were taking away a whole generation of sewers—meaning Singer customers.

It made little sense for the company to keep paying taxes year after year on 120 square miles of trees in Louisiana that it no longer seemed to need. So in 1937 Singer sold off a small piece of its land—six thousand acres—to the Tendall Lumber Company. Two years later, it sold Chicago Mill the right to cut all the rest—about seventy-three thousand acres of mostly virgin forest.

In 1939, after building railroad tracks from Tallulah out to the forest, Chicago Mill started logging the west side of the Tensas River. The railroad made everything portable—even families. Tiny prefabricated one-room shacks were pitched onto flatcars and hauled by train into the woods, where they were unloaded and set down in rows on a patch of cleared land near the cutting site. White workers lived on one end of a row, and blacks—who outnumbered whites and did the hardest work—on the other. When the job was finished in one part of the forest, families helped pick up their own homes and heave them back onto the train to be hauled off to the next work site.

The hoots of Barred Owls, the electric chatter of tree frogs, the hair-raising cries of wolves, and the tooting calls of Ivory-billed Woodpeckers were soon drowned out by the grinding, growling machines. "Those woods were *loud*," recalls Gene Laird, who grew up in the forest during those years. "The train whistle was earsplitting—four blasts meant 'get off the track.' Axes rang, people yelled and whoop-whooped to be heard, and behind it all the crawler tractors hauling logs were always growling."

The loggers worked seven days a week from dawn till

THE SANTEE COOPER PROJECT

About the same time Chicago Mill began cutting the Singer Tract, the Ivory-bill suffered another blow in South Carolina. On April 18, 1939, loggers began cutting huge cypress and live oak trees in the floodplain of the Santee River to make way for a dam. The idea was to back the river's water up into two lakes behind the dam so that South Carolinians could swim, boat, and fish. Building the dam would also create jobs at a time when many people were out of work. Some of the river's water would flow through a "spillway," or door, at the dam, turning turbines to create electric power.

Families who lived in the forested area along the river were moved out and told to become farmers. They were given one hundred free chickens and loans to buy seed. Homes, churches, schools, and even cemeteries were moved out of the way. On November 12, 1941, spillway doors were closed against the river and lakes Marion and Moultrie began to fill up behind the dam.

Though Jim Tanner didn't find Ivory-bills when he explored the Santee River swamp in 1937, he was convinced they were still there. The Santee Cooper Project, as the dam was called, removed the last sizable habitat for the Ivory-billed Woodpecker in South Carolina.

MOVING DAY, WISNER, MISS.

(top) A portable shack in an early-twentieth-century Mississippi logging camp is lifted up on a railroad car with a woman still in residence

(bottom) Loggers at the Singer Tract in 1939, before most African American workers left to fight in World War II or work in factories in the North

dusk—or from "can" till "can't," as they put it. They worked in the rain and they worked in the cold. When the ground was too soggy for sawyers to stand on, they drove a long wedge called a kickboard into the trunk of a tree. A man hopped up onto each end. From their dry perch, the duo counted out "One, two, three!" and began to push and pull a twelve-foot-long crosscut blade to the rhythm. First it bit into the thick gray trunk. Then it entered the sapwood, slicing back and forth through wood that was laid down during the early part of the twentieth century. Then it reached the heartwood, penetrating wood dating from the Civil War and earlier, until the tree began to sway, gently at first and then teetering violently, until there was a last long dying crack. Then the tree came screaming down, tearing through the limbs of trees beside it, striking the earth with a boom that shook the forest for a few final seconds. Bouncing once or twice, it at last lay still and then was set upon by ax-wielding men who chopped the trunk into neat logs. The logs were dragged away two at a time by tractor-driven "skidders" to boxcars that were always waiting at the rail, doors wide open like the mouths of babies waiting to be fed.

THE SWAMP DATE

And so the race was on: could the last Ivory-bill forest be saved before the Lord God bird ran out of food? With the wilderness shrinking every day, Audubon's John Baker flew into action. Early in 1940 he got Louisiana politicians to introduce a bill into Congress to create a "Tensas Swamp National Park." If passed into law, this bill, numbered H.R. 9720, would stop the cutting and protect up to sixty thousand acres—what was left of the Singer Tract. The U.S. government would take over the land and run it as a park, complete with visitor programs. One catch was that the bill didn't propose allocating any money for the government to buy the land—it would have to be raised. Baker knew the bill would be hard to pass, since few northern politicians would care much about a forest in the Deep South. Majestic mountainous places like Yosemite or Rocky Mountain National Park were one thing, but who would care about making a park out of a swamp in Louisiana?

Baker wrote to President Franklin D. Roosevelt asking him to support the bill. He also asked the governor of Louisiana to find money to buy the land and wrote to Chicago Mill's president requesting a meeting to talk about selling the company's logging rights. The company was slow to answer. When a reply finally came, Chicago Mill's president said he doubted that anything could be worked out that would satisfy both the company and the woodpecker. "That remains to be seen," Baker scrawled defiantly on the envelope.

In Louisiana, gum and oak trees kept thundering to the ground throughout the summer and fall of 1940. Baker suspected Chicago Mill was working at breakneck speed, trying to get the trees cut before a park could be established. Four hundred miles away, at a small college deep in the Appalachian Mountains, Dr. James Tanner, now a biology professor at East Tennessee State, was also worried about what was going on at the Singer Tract. Besides wanting to see for himself, he had fallen in love, and he wanted to show slender, red-haired professor Nancy Sheedy the most important place in his life before it was too late.

The young couple drove to Tallulah over the Christmas break and were soon wearing hip boots and hiking into John's Bayou, where they heard Ivory-bills yapping but couldn't find them. From time to time the low rumble of tractors was faintly audible in the background, but the crew sounded far away. When sunlight began to fade, they hiked out. Jim thought he knew the tree where the Ivory-bills would roost that night. They could find it in the morning.

At 4:30 a.m., Nancy was waiting on the sidewalk in front of the hotel when Jim pulled up, breakfast and lunch packed in fresh paper sacks on the seat. When they reached the forest, the sky was still starry and the woods were pulsing with the night language of crickets and frogs and Barred Owls. The air smelled damp and earthy. They entered the woods without a flashlight and made a pact not to talk unless absolutely necessary. They stopped often to listen for birds as the first faint light of dawn appeared. Amazingly, Jim went directly to the roosting tree he had talked about the day before. "I don't know how he knew where he was," Nancy recalled more than sixty years later. "It all looked the same to me."

They sat down side by side on a wet log and waited in silence as the sun climbed above the treetops and the forest stirred to life. For an hour they kept their eyes fixed on an oval hole near the top of the tree. Finally they were rewarded when a pair of Ivory-bills appeared. "The male came out first, just about the time the sun topped the trees," Nancy later recalled. "He crawled out of the roost hole, clung to the side of the tree, and stretched and preened . . . I remember that gorgeous crimson crest and that white bill . . . and those incredible fiery yellow eyes. What a striking creature."

Jim and Nancy were married the next summer and soon settled back into the routine of preparing lectures and grading papers. But then something happened that changed everything. On December 7, 1941, Japanese planes attacked Pearl Harbor. The next day the United States declared war on Japan, and three days later was at war with Germany and Italy. The United States had entered World War II.

Tanner hoped that habitat could be saved for breeding Ivory-bills at Greenlea Bend, the one part of the Singer Tract remaining as it once was

Two weeks after the Pearl Harbor attack, the Tanners drove back to Louisiana for one last look at the Singer Tract before Jim had to report for military duty. They explored the swamp together on foot and horseback for nearly two weeks. Though the bayous were swollen with rainwater, they were able to reach all the familiar Ivory-bill spots but one.

Things had changed dramatically in the course of a year. Now the machines growled constantly and the scarred land was a trash heap of lopped-off limbs and tree stubs. Jim and Nancy could find only two Ivory-bills left—both females—and maybe heard a third at another part of the Singer Tract known as Mack's Bayou.

Just before returning home, Jim

convinced Sam Alexander, the head of Chicago Mill and Lumber Company's logging department, to take a walk with him through the forest. Tanner patiently pointed out the kinds of trees Ivory-bills used most. Together they examined sheets of stripped bark hanging loose from Ivory-bill food trees. Tanner even showed Alexander specific trees still being used by the few birds left. Alexander paid close attention but said little. Finally he shook his head. Those trees still had a lot of good wood in them, he said. He didn't see how he could leave many of them standing.

Tanner feared that the forest was doomed—soon the big trees would be separated into fragments of forest that would be too small to feed even a single pair of Ivory-bills. The bombs at Pearl Harbor had also destroyed the bill to make a Tensas Swamp National Park—no one was thinking about anything but war now.

The only hope left for the Singer Tract was to try to save one last big intact piece of the Ivory-bill forest before it all turned to sawdust. Chicago Mill had already cut the best sweet gum at John's Bayou, so that was gone. Tanner thought there might still be time to save Greenlea Bend. Almost all the original parts of the forest ecosystem were still there—the cypress sloughs, the oak ridges, the cypress-ringed lakes—there might even be a surviving pair of Ivory-bills that could rebuild a family and save the species. Tanner wrote to John Baker, "Greenlea Bend is small compared with the entire [Singer] tract, but it is the gem of it all; it is the part that I would rather see preserved more than any other."

When the Tanners arrived back home in Tennessee, they found a letter waiting for them that began with the word "Greetings." Jim was now Lieutenant AG James Tanner of the United States Navy. Soon he would be ordered to report for radar training in Brunswick, Maine. Jim Tanner was ready to serve his country and go. What he didn't know was that he wouldn't see the Singer Tract again for forty-five years.

WAR IN A BOX

To the Chicago Mill and Lumber Company, World War II came in a box. The armed forces needed boxes to hold airplanes, shells, tanks, medicine, and dry food to be shipped overseas. Overnight, Chicago Mill could sell all the boxes it could make to the

EXECUTIVE ORDER 8802

In 1940 the NAACP's magazine Crisis *ran a story titled "Warplanes: Negro Americans May Not Build Them, Repair Them or Fly Them, but They Must Help Pay for Them (with Taxes)." Fewer than 1 percent of the jobs in airplane factories were held by blacks. Black leaders threatened to organize a huge march on Washington demanding good, high-paying defense jobs unless President Roosevelt did something about it first.*

The pressure worked. On June 25, 1941, President Roosevelt passed Executive Order 8802 setting up the Committee on Fair Employment Practices to ensure that blacks got their share of the factory jobs. Roosevelt said, "There shall be no discrimination in the employment of workers in defense industries or government because of race, creed, color, or national origin." After that, doors flew open for blacks in shipyards and factories. And many black women and men from southern states like Louisiana walked through them.

War Department. There was only one problem: with so many young men drafted into service, who would be left to cut the trees?

The problem was severe in northeastern Louisiana, where there were far more blacks than whites. Before 1940, there were only 5,000 African Americans in all the U.S. Army. By 1944 there were 700,000. The need to manufacture war supplies created factory jobs in northern cities that lured black women and men away from their plows and fields in the South. Between 1940 and 1950, more than a thousand blacks left Madison Parish, many of them laborers who had worked in the woods and fields.

In March 1942, Chicago Mill's president, James F. Griswold, showed up at Audubon House in New York City, finally ready to talk with Baker about the Singer land. The two men bent over maps and talked about how much money it would take to buy Greenlea Bend. The price they came up with to save four thousand acres was about $200,000. The men got along surprisingly well, and the meeting gave Baker a glimmer of hope. "Mr. Griswold has just been with me here at Audubon House," he wrote to Tanner. "He was most agreeable and sympathetic in his attitude."

And so, as the clock ticked down the final minutes of the chance to save a big scrap of the Singer Tract, things seemed to be falling into place. Louisiana governor Sam H. Jones came up with $200,000 to buy the land. He joined the governors of Tennessee, Arkansas, and Mississippi in writing a letter to Chicago Mill and the Singer company, urging them to sell their rights so the trees could be preserved. Officials of the Roosevelt Administration agreed to state in writing that the United States didn't need the lumber at the Singer Tract to win the war.

Baker found a publisher to produce a book of Jim Tanner's report on the Ivory-billed Woodpecker so more people could know how important this issue was. With only a few weeks left before he had to leave for the Navy, Jim set up a card table in his living room and plunked his typewriter on it. He worked day and night to finish his manuscript.

Finally, Chicago Mill consented to an all-or-nothing meeting with everyone who was pressuring it to stop cutting at the Singer Tract. The date was set for December 8, 1943, in Chicago. As the meeting date drew near, Baker ordered an Audubon worker named Richard Pough to quietly slip down to the Singer Tract and look for Ivory-bills "so that no one could say there weren't any down there." Pough's instructions were to avoid all Chicago Mill people if he could—in effect, he was a spy.

Baker probably woke up on the day of the meeting with a cautious feeling of hope. With the labor shortage and the money that had been raised, maybe the companies would at least sell the rights to Greenlea Bend. But something else was happening that Baker didn't know. Chicago Mill was no longer short of workers in Louisiana. Help had arrived—from an unimaginable place.

Entrance to the Chicago Mill and
Lumber Company mill, Tallulah,
Louisiana

CHAPTER TWELVE
VISITING WITH ETERNITY

When the last individual of a race of living things breathes no more, another heaven and another earth must pass before such a one can be again.

—William Beebe (1906)

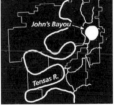

The Ivory-bill made its last stand within the Singer Tract, at John's Bayou, once the site of Camp Ephilus and the birthplace of Sonny Boy

Madison Parish, Louisiana — 1943-1944

TWELVE-YEAR-OLD BILLY FOUGHT SCUFFED HIS BOOT IN THE RED DUST AS HE WAITED for his school bus to come where Sharkey Road crossed the Chicago Mill railroad tracks. It was a late autumn day in 1943. The leaves were already starting to turn. Billy and his ten-year-old brother, Bobby, were new to the countryside. After their mother had died, their dad had moved them from Tallulah to take a job driving a spur train for the Chicago Mill and Lumber Company. Now they were "swamp rats," living in Chicago Mill's portable logging camp and playing and fishing in the bayous. But they still had to go to school, and so there they stood, alone, waiting for the bus.

Billy looked up when he heard a motor. Instead of the bus, he saw a black truck, filled with men. The truck stopped, and about twenty husky young white men were ushered out by armed guards. The men wore identical blue jumpsuits, navy-blue caps, and armbands with the big letters "PW." Whatever they were saying to each other, it sure didn't sound like English.

Billy had heard the grownups talking about this, but it hadn't seemed possible. German soldiers, the enemy—*Nazis*—had come to work in their woods. But it was true. Day after day, the truck arrived at the crossroads and the young men jumped out, some carrying hand-carved wooden lunchboxes. Enemy soldiers from the very same army that was trying to kill American soldiers halfway around the world—soldiers from Tallulah, even—stood around the clearing, stretching and chatting for a few minutes each day until they were led into the woods or sent out to work on the railroad tracks. One day, one of them actually beckoned to Bobby and offered him a candy bar. As Bobby slowly reached out his hand for it, Billy grabbed his arm. "Don't eat it!" he hissed. "It might be poison!" The German got down on one knee to look directly at Bobby. He said, in English, "Please take it. I have a boy at home, too. You remind me of him."

The German on the other end of that candy bar had seen a lot of the world in the past two years. He had been captured in North Africa, where he had fought as part of an elite German unit called the Afrika Korps. Its mission was to conquer Egypt and seize control of the Suez Canal between the Red Sea and Mediterranean so that the Axis forces—Germany, Japan, and Italy—could command the oil fields of the Middle East.

Instead, caught in a trap between U.S. and British forces, the German soldiers were defeated. Many were killed and a multitude—hundreds of thousands of Axis troops—were captured. Since British jails were already full, the British asked the United States to take them, and the War Department reluctantly agreed.

The prisoners were marched onto big, flat-decked "Liberty Ships" that sailed from North Africa to Scotland and then on to Liverpool, England. Most prisoners probably assumed they had reached their destination, but there was yet another body of water to cross—the Atlantic. Weeks later, when the great ships approached New York City, all prisoners were ordered on deck to see the Statue of Liberty and the giant skyscrapers take shape on the western horizon. Many stared in open-mouthed disbelief, for their officers had told them New York had been destroyed. Some thought it was a trick—a Hollywood film set.

In New York the men were put on trains and transported under guard to prison camps throughout the United States. It surprised some German prisoners that they were allowed to sit in cars reserved for whites, while blacks, who were fighting for America, sat in segregated cars. In all, about twenty thousand prisoners of war journeyed to Louisiana, where they were then sent to one of four main camps. On

August 14, 1943, the first three hundred Afrika Korps prisoners, still tanned from the African sun, marched into Camp Ruston, a prison camp about forty miles from Tallulah.

The next month, the War Department announced that the POWs would be available to Louisiana planters and other companies that needed laborers. Employers would have to pay them a small salary, transport them between their prison camps and the work sites, provide guards, and feed them. The Tallulah fairground was wrapped in barbed wire for 505 German prisoners, who promptly set up their own kitchen, bakery, and library.

Chicago Mill was one of the first companies to snap up the cheap labor, sending trucks to pick up the POWs at the camp and drive them out to the Singer Tract each morning. And that was why Bobby Fought, standing on a red dirt road near Tallulah, Louisiana, found himself on the other end of a candy bar offered by a Nazi soldier.

Some of the German prisoners picked up crosscut saws and took on the hard work usually done only by black workers. Others chopped logs or loaded freight cars or worked on the railroad. Those with professional training became mechanics and engineers. None of them had ever seen forests anything like the thick, tangled woods of the South. One complained, "When we Germans hear the word 'forest' we think of the beauty of our homeland . . . [Here] a thicket of thorns blocks the way to the trees. You have to hack your way in." And they

THE ENEMY AMONG US

About 375,000 German prisoners worked and lived in forty-four states between 1943 and 1946. They labored in canneries, foundries, quarries, forests, mills, and mines. They picked cotton, dug potatoes, and harvested corn.

They marched into camps as hardened Nazis, but most became less and less militant as the months wore on. They were fed well and quickly gained weight. They seemed to like outdoor work and were glad not to be in prison. Guiltily, local teams played against them in football and soccer. Prison officials, at first nervous, relaxed their guard and let them supervise their own men at work. The POWs baked good bread, which they sold at prison stores. Americans stood in line to buy the things they carved. In Louisiana, one prisoner carved a fine chess set. At Tallulah, a German made a fine violin from scrap. At Camp Livingston, one man made a collapsible model house. Few tried to escape, and many returned to the United States to live after the war.

hated the insects. Wrote another, "Who does not know these little red stitches . . . itching and biting like hundreds of ants? . . . There seems to be no medicine against the bite of a spider like a point of a needle."

The Germans were like a gift from heaven to the Chicago Mill and Lumber Company. Now it could make money three ways in one project: it could clear the Singer Tract with workers who were practically free; it could sell as many boxes as it could make to the ravenous War Department; and it could sell the cutover land to ru-

German prisoners of war cut trees in the South

ral families who wanted cheap farmland. Chicago Mill didn't even have to clean up the mess it had made. "The waste, you couldn't believe it," recalls Gene Laird. "If you stood at a cut-down tree and it didn't measure three feet around, they'd just leave it on the ground."

With new muscle from the prisoners, the 45-foot-long conveyor belt that delivered logs to a giant toothed blade at the Tallulah sawmill ran twenty-four hours a day. Log by log, two hundred years of southern history was ground into yellow dust. The mysterious, howling Tensas swamp forest, nightmare of planter families, was tamed by a single machine. From time to time the blade jammed on balls of shot from the Civil War still buried in the logs coming through. When that happened, the log was tossed aside, a switch was flicked, and the blade ground on.

Against those whirring teeth the last great Ivory-bill forest collapsed day by day—and with it went Chicago Mill's interest in saving even a single tree.

"WE ARE JUST MONEY GRUBBERS"

At noon on Wednesday, December 8, 1943, a group of men stomped in from the Chicago winter, squirmed out of their overcoats, placed their hats on racks, and shuffled into Chicago Mill's downtown boardroom. Seated around the table were important representatives from the federal government, the southern states, the Audubon Society, and the Singer company. After introductions, the group quickly settled down to business. Audubon president John Baker's report tells what happened next: "[Chicago Mill] refused to cooperate in any way, and said that it would not enter into any deal unless forced to. The Chairman said, among other things, 'We are just money grubbers. We are not concerned, as are you folks, with ethical considerations.' They would not help in any way with the creation of a park or refuge 'unless forced to do so.' "

The Singer company's position was the same. It no longer cared about the trees on its property—what happened to them was up to Chicago Mill. Singer wasn't even making sewing machines during the war—its manufacturing equipment was now cranking out gun sights and triggers.

The bad news didn't stop there. Richard Pough, the man Baker had sent to Louisiana to find Ivory-bills, telegrammed that after three weeks of searching he hadn't been able to find a single bird. What he *had* seen turned his stomach. "It is sickening to see what a waste a lumber company can make of what was a beautiful forest," Pough wrote to Baker. "I watched them cutting the last stand of the finest sweet gum on Monday. One log was six feet in diameter at the butt."

But three weeks later, as freezing rain popped onto the forest floor and spread a fine glaze of ice over the bare limbs above, Pough's luck changed. From a logging road at John's Bayou, he heard at last the "kent, kent" cry he had been awaiting for so long. Hopping over tractor gashes, he chased the sound through a wasteland of mashed limbs to an ash tree in a small section of the forest still not cut. He raised his eyes and finally found his trophy—a female Ivory-billed Woodpecker. Her well-used roost tree was riddled with six large holes. Though it was well into January, she still had no mate.

Pough sadly watched the bird feed for a while, then hiked into Tallulah to telegram Baker in New York. "I have been able to locate only a single female and feel reasonably sure there are no other birds here," he dictated. He soon followed it with another message: "I really fear the area will be cut any day."

Baker kept trying to stop the logging and save the land. He wrote letters to magazine writers and politicians, hoping to put pressure on Chicago Mill. Even if the Ivory-bills were almost gone, he argued, wouldn't a scrap of the last virgin forest left in the Mississippi River delta still be worth saving? Didn't we owe that to future generations of southerners, at least? But the nation could hear only war. Chicago Mill's saw whined on without pause as more and more boxcars, sometimes fifty at a time, lined up for the wood. The War Department needed plywood cut from sweet gums to make gasoline tanks for jet fighters. They wanted boxes to hold shells. Even the British army had a special need for the last Ivory-bill forest. A history of the Chicago Mill and Lumber Company says, "The Tallulah plant was so busy making tea chests for supplying the English army with its tea that they had a regular production line which ended in three box cars sitting side by side on the railroad siding tracks."

Several members of the Audubon Society's New York City staff journeyed to John's Bayou as if they were saying farewell to a friend with a terminal illness. Baker himself went to see the bird, as did Roger Tory Peterson. Don Eckelberry, who illustrated Audubon field guides, bundled up his outdoor clothes and sketch pads and boarded a southbound train as soon as he read Richard Pough's disastrous news. Eckelberry was determined to sketch and paint the last Ivory-bill before it died.

Eckelberry arrived in Louisiana in April 1944. He was welcomed by Jesse Laird, a local warden who had helped Jim Tanner in the final year of his study. One late afternoon, Laird and Eckelberry reached the ash tree where the female Ivory-bill had been roosting every night. The men sat silently on a log and waited as sunlight slipped away. At 6:25 they heard her rap on a tree in the distance. There was no answer. She called for about twenty minutes more, as if beckoning a mate. Finally, wrote Eckelberry, "she came trumpeting into the roost, her big wings cleaving the air in strong, direct flight, and she alighted with one magnificent upward swoop. Looking about wildly with her hysterical pale eyes, tossing her head from side to side, her black crest erect to the point of leaning forward, she hitched up the tree at a gallop, trumpeting all the way."

With too little light left to sketch, Eckelberry just watched, awestruck, until dark. He felt like he was staring at eternity. This single unmated female was all that remained of the Lord God bird that had commanded America's great swamp forests for thousands of years. She was the sole known remainder of a life-form that had predated Columbus, or Christ, or even Native Americans. The arrow-like flight, the two-note whacks that echoed through gloomy forests, the ability to peel entire trees— all that was left of these ancient behaviors was now right before his eyes.

Eckelberry returned to the tree most days for the next two weeks, riding to the Sharkey plantation in Jesse Laird's jeep and then hiking half a mile into the forest with his paper, brushes, paint, pencils, sketch pads, and binoculars. He sketched at dawn and dusk, when the bird was at her roost tree, because he couldn't begin to keep up with her as she flew over the forest. He liked to think he was "waking up with her" and "putting her to bed." Sometimes he lost track of time until he realized he was sitting in darkness. Then he hoped the moon would come up bright so he could find his way home.

On one of those days, Billy and Bobby Fought were skipping stones off the bridge at the Sharkey plantation road with two other boys when Mr. Laird's jeep drove up. The door opened and a stranger got out, carrying a huge sketch pad and a box of pencils. He was slender and dignified-looking, and he walked with a limp. The boys clustered around. He introduced himself as Don Eckelberry and said he was hiking to a tree to sketch the last Ivory-billed Woodpecker. Did they want to go with him? Mr. Laird said they should, it was their chance to see a great bird maybe no one would ever see again. "You'll have to be quiet," Mr. Laird said. The Fought brothers quickly stepped forward as the other boys turned back to throwing rocks. "Will it be okay with your parents?" the stranger asked. "Yessir," replied Billy Fought. "We don't have to ask when to go into the woods."

So the two boys and Eckelberry waded and splashed to the gnarled ash tree and sat down on a log, a boy on either side of the artist. He sketched everything in sight as they waited. He drew the ash tree, a wolf, the flowers, the birds, even Bobby Fought. He couldn't seem to stop, and they had never seen anyone who could draw so fast or so well. And then, around suppertime, the air seemed to stand still as the Ivory-bill winged in. She rapped on the tree with her gleaming beak, hopped up, went into the nest, stuck her head back out as if to say good night, and then disappeared. The artist told the brothers that he hoped they could understand how special this moment was and that he hoped somehow they would remember it always, even though they were young. He drew as he spoke, and the great bird seemed to come to life on his pad.

"I've never been quite the same since," says Billy Fought, now in his seventies. "I'll never forget Mr. Eckelberry, or that bird, or that day, as long as I live."

A WINDSTORM

After finishing his sketches, Don Eckelberry made one final visit to the ash tree. He probably wished he hadn't. Overnight, the portable railroad had moved the German prisoners much closer to the roost tree. He observed their work for a while and

Twelve-year-old Gene Laird may have been the last person to spot an Ivory-bill in the United States

then turned away. Later, he wrote, "I watched as one tree came screaming down and cared to see no more."

It has been written that Don Eckelberry had the last "authenticated" sighting—that is, by an expert—of an Ivory-billed Woodpecker in the United States. That may be true, but he wasn't the last person to see it at the Singer Tract. Gene Laird, the twelve-year-old son of Jesse, helped his family by driving their cattle on horseback through the grand old trees. The trees at Singer were so big that their wide crowns drew together to form a leafy shield at the top, blocking sunlight from reaching the ground. Because young trees couldn't grow in the shade, spaces on the ground between the giants were wide enough for Gene to drive cattle through, giving them exercise and letting them graze on switch cane that grew beneath the trees.

There was only one small detour in his daily route. His father, having worked with Tanner and having grown to love the Ivory-billed Woodpecker himself, had Gene ride past the old ash tree and check in on the last female Ivory-bill every day. Gene did it for about a week after Don Eckelberry left, sometimes stopping to keep the bird company for a while. Since Chicago Mill was cutting only sweet gum and oak trees, they had passed over the ash tree and moved on. The female was still there, rapping and calling for a mate that was no more. And then, as Gene Laird remembered many years later, "one day I went by there and the ash had blown down in a windstorm. She was gone. And I never saw an Ivory-billed Woodpecker again."

Ivory-bill country in eastern Cuba

CHAPTER THIRTEEN
CARPINTERO REAL:
BETWEEN SCIENCE AND MAGIC

The Ivory-bill is a messenger of the old days from the great forest that covered our land.
It is a link between the people of North America and Cuba. It lives between
science and magic.

—Giraldo Alayón, Cuban biologist who has seen the Ivory-bill

Mid-1980s

Eastern Cuba, 1985–1987

THE CLOSEST RELATIVE TO THE IVORY-BILLED WOODPECKER OF THE UNITED STATES IS the Cuban Ivory-bill (*Campephilus principalis bairdii*). Most experts believe these birds are simply two populations of the same species that became separated long ago. Museum specimens of Ivory-bills from the two countries look the same, except that the Cuban birds tend to be a little smaller and the white line that runs down each side of the body starts a bit closer to the ear on the Cuban Ivory-bill. During the years when Jim Tanner was exploring the Singer Tract, scientists thought that the Cuban and U.S. birds were two separate species, but opinion changed around 1950, when biologists concluded that the slight differences in appearance wouldn't keep birds from the two populations from interbreeding if they ever came in contact.

Ivory-bills have been rapidly disappearing in Cuba, too, but because they have been seen there much more recently than in the United States, there's a ghost of a chance that a few birds still inhabit the rugged, rust-colored mountains of the east. Every year, teams of searchers thread their way through those jagged peaks, hauling camping gear and scientific equipment up over the powdery trails to look for them.

Cuba was home to its own population of Ivory-bills, known only to a few ornithologists. Clearing of lowland forests reduced the Cuban Ivory-bill's habitat to the eastern mountains

CAMPEPHILUS PRINCIPALIS BAIRDII CASSIN

CORREOS DE CUBA 2 ¢

NAVIDAD 1961 - 62.

The Ivory-bill was featured on this now-rare Cuban stamp, issued in 1962

When they stop from time to time to gasp for breath, they send recordings of the old Cornell tape out into the mountain air, hoping an Ivory-bill will answer. So far, none has.

Since 1985, guides and scientists have spent more than forty thousand hours looking for the bird Cubans call *Carpintero real*—the Royal Carpenter. And in all that time there have been only nine glimpses of an Ivory-bill, adding up to maybe two minutes of time. The longest sighting lasted only about twenty seconds. There are no photos.

The most determined of the searchers has seen the Ivory-bill four times and has organized the expeditions that have been most successful at tracking it down. Giraldo Alayón has studied the great bird for more than thirty years, collecting scientific information and folklore in a series of files and journals. He has become as important to the Ivory-bill in Cuba as James Tanner was in the United States. He is also Cuba's national spider expert.

The son of a lensmaker, Alayón grew up in the town of San Antonio de los Baños during the years of the Cuban Revolution. Just about everything changed in San Antonio in those days except for one thing—the movies. Even as the United States was being cursed as Cuba's enemy, even as governments were bracing for possible conflict, the Casino theater downtown kept right on showing American films.

Giraldo's future snapped into focus one Saturday night in December 1960, when he went to the movies with his sister and two friends to see a film based on Jules

Verne's *Journey to the Center of the Earth*. For two hours, eleven-year-old Giraldo sat wide-eyed as four American actors and a duck named Gertrude probed the core of the earth itself. He stared as Alex—played by Pat Boone—lowered himself into the chimney of a volcano. He held his breath as the giant reptile *Dimetrodon* nearly carried off Arlene Dahl. And when the great geologist Professor Oliver Lindenbrook, played by James Mason, informed his students that "the spirit of man cannot be stopped," Giraldo Alayón knew for sure that he wanted to be a scientist.

After high school, Giraldo enrolled in Havana University, first studying physics and then switching to biology. Spiders were his passion. Their diversity of color and form and behavior fascinated him. No two seemed alike. He was never happier than when he was crawling through a cave or inspecting rocks, logs, bushes, or crevices for spiders. One night in the winter of 1970, after a spider-collecting field trip to the eastern mountains, Alayón relaxed contentedly on a log before a crackling campfire, listening to neighboring peasants tell stories of a big white-billed woodpecker of the deep forest. The way they spoke made it hard to know whether it was real or legendary. They swore it had mystical qualities, calling it the guardian spirit of the forest. Alayón's professor, Fernando Ciyas, declared that he, too, had once seen the skin of this sacred bird nailed to the back of a peasant's door, its wings stretched into the shape of a cross.

Alayón was fascinated. A huge, white-billed *spiritual* woodpecker? Later he returned to the area to collect more stories—accounts that deepened his interest. Woodsmen told him that this woodpecker's bones could be ground into a powder to keep evil spirits away. Others repeated that the bird's spirit guarded the forest. The only problem was that hardly anyone he interviewed had actually *seen* this creature they called *Carpintero real*. Did it really exist?

Alayón went to museums and libraries, just as Jim Tanner had in the United States, to pore through books and specimen cabinets for any scraps of information at all about the Ivory-bill. There was precious little. The Spaniards who had ruled Cuba

NATURAL CUBA

Cuba is a big island, about the size of Pennsylvania, accounting for about half the land mass of all the islands in the West Indies. Cuba's landscape is extremely varied. There is a desert, a huge swamp much like the Everglades, and three mountain ranges with peaks almost as high as any in the eastern United States.

Because Cuba is an island, many species evolved there. Twenty-one bird species are found only in Cuba, including the world's smallest bird—the Bee Hummingbird. Half of Cuba's 580 spider species are endemic—found only there. Cuba has twenty-five different species of scorpions, its own crocodile, and twenty-five endemic butterfly species.

Many birds that migrate to the United States to breed in the warm, buggy months spend most of their year in Cuba.

for four hundred years had seemingly overlooked it. No scientist mentioned it at all until the 1860s, and in the century that followed there were only two detailed reports.

After 1900, most of Cuba's forests were cleared for growing sugarcane. The few scientists who knew about the Ivory-bill worried that it had become extinct in Cuba. But in the 1940s and 1950s, two U.S.-led expeditions rediscovered the species. The second quest, led by scientists George and Barbara Lamb, found six mated pairs in a hidden mountain forest known as Bandilero. This land was owned by two U.S. companies. The Lambs believed that if a preserve could be established, enough breeding birds might remain to rebuild the population and save the species.

THE CUBAN REVOLUTION

All during the 1950s a storm had been gathering in Cuba. A growing number of Cubans were tired of having their country ruled by Fulgencio Batista, a corrupt dictator who allowed wealth to become concentrated in the hands of a few. Some thought the United States had too much control over Cuba's economy, culture, and land. During that decade a young lawyer, Fidel Castro, the son of a wealthy sugar planter, led rebel forces against the government from Ivory-bill country—remote mountain outposts in the eastern part of the island. The rebels took over in 1959, and Castro became the head of the government.

Relations between the United States and Cuba froze solid when Castro declared himself a Communist and accepted support from the United States' global enemy—the Soviet Union. In 1960 Cuba took over all U.S. property on the island, and most U.S. workers scrambled for home. President John F. Kennedy quickly outlawed U.S. trade with Cuba, and most contact between U.S. and Cuban scientists—including research on the Ivory-billed Woodpecker—all but stopped for more than three decades.

But the Cuban Revolution changed everything. In 1959, after the dictatorship of Fulgencio Batista had collapsed and rebels took control, most Americans left in haste and the Cuban government took over the land at Bandilero. Once again the phantom woodpecker seemed to slip away into the twilight of legend. There were no more Ivory-bill reports at all until one day in 1968 when a biologist named Orlando Garrido happened upon a lone female while collecting reptiles at a mountain forest known as Cupeyal. From its safe vantage point high in a pine tree, the great glossy bird had hitched its way around from behind the trunk to get a clear look at the startled Garrido. It cocked its head and inspected him for a while, uttered a sharp yelp, and shot off across a valley. Garrido had no idea that the Ivory-bill was on the brink of extinction, but he did recall that he had a book about it back in his Havana office. He remembered photos of a baby bird on a man's arm and head. These, of course, were the famous photos in Jim Tanner's book. Garrido then wrote about his discovery.

Almost a decade later, in the late 1970s, Giraldo Alayón read Garrido's report and questioned him about the Ivory-bill he had seen. The two scientists began to converse excitedly at the University of Havana about organizing a new expedition to search for it. Since the older and better-known Garrido was often pulled away to lead field trips throughout Cuba, Alayón took the lead. Again and again, he traveled to the mountains, interviewing country people, listening to more stories, and mapping the places they told him about. Finding this lost bird became an obsession. Like so many researchers before him, dark-eyed, mustachioed Giraldo Alayón felt himself drawn toward this elusive creature that seemed to exist in a dimension all its own.

SWIMMING AGAINST THE TIDE

While many Americans who lived in Cuba fled the island after the revolution, one man was trying to get *in*. Dr. Lester Short, Curator of Ornithology at the American Museum of Natural History, was a stocky man whose broad face was fringed with a whitening beard. He probably knew more about woodpeckers than anyone else in the world. His book *Woodpeckers of the World* was a bible for ornithologists. There were few woodpeckers on earth that Lester Short hadn't seen. One was the Ivory-bill.

For twelve years Short tried in vain to get permission from the U.S. and Cuban governments to search for the Ivory-bill in Cuba. He filled out endless forms and wrote countless letters. But always there was another form to fill out, always another official to consult, always someone else who had to grant the final permission.

But then, in August 1984, Short received an unexpected call from a man who introduced himself as Comandante Universo Sánchez Alvarez, director of Cuba's Bureau of Flora, Fauna, and Protected Areas. Sánchez Alvarez wished to invite Dr. Short to Cuba to help search for the Ivory-billed Woodpecker. Sánchez Alvarez hoped that if the bird could be found again, Short's worldwide reputation might help Cuban scientists make a case for creating a large nature preserve in the forest to protect it.

Short arrived in February 1985, along with Cornell sound

ORLANDO GARRIDO

Dr. Orlando Garrido, the Cuban biologist who saw the Ivory-bill in 1968, was at one time a world-class tennis player. But even in a big match, biology was never far from his mind. In 1959, while representing Cuba in the Davis Cup tennis competition, Garrido was about to serve the ball to his Australian opponent when he noticed a huge beetle crawling slowly across the court in front of him. It was a magnificent specimen. Raising his hand, Garrido signaled the referee to stop play, and as the crowd watched in amazement, he walked to the sidelines, found an empty tennis ball can, went back to the court, and carefully scooped up the insect and placed it inside. Only when the lid was tightly secured did he walk back to resume play.

technician George Reynard. Their guide was Giraldo Alayón. Alayón led the Americans to Cupeyal, where Orlando Garrido had last seen the bird seventeen years earlier. The explorers pushed themselves to cover twelve miles a day, often leaning into a hard, driving rain. They saw no birds, but now and again they came upon trees whose bark had been scaled back, suggesting that maybe a lone Ivory-bill had passed through.

On the morning of the fifth day an old man rode into their camp on horseback. Dismounting, he introduced himself as Felipe Montero Rodríguez, a logger who had been cutting trees in those mountains for thirty years. He said he had information for the men seeking the *Carpintero real*. Explaining that he had kept track of the bird because he loved it, Señor Rodríguez reported that Ivory-bills had declined steadily throughout the 1950s, 1960s, and 1970s until they seemed to be completely gone in 1977—or so he thought. But just a few weeks before, while he was working, he was startled to hear the sound of a familiar crack of bone against wood. Dropping his blade at his feet, he crashed through the forest at a full sprint until he saw it—a bird bigger than the Cuban Crow, black-and-white, with a black crest pointing forward—a female Ivory-bill! He said the tree was only about five miles away from where they were now.

That was good enough for Alayón and Short. They folded their tents, struck camp, and followed the old man's hand-drawn map. They searched for another three days without success, but they had no doubt that his detailed story had the ring of truth. Lester Short returned to New York convinced that there were still Ivory-bills in Cuba. Finding them would be like finding a needle in a haystack—and one that moved at that. But they were out there. The team had simply not yet found the right place to search.

MARCH 16

The old peasant squinted at the picture of the bird Giraldo Alayón had handed him, and then smiled. His smile split into a grin when Alayón clicked on his tape recorder and the rapid succession of toots and yaps came pouring out. These were sounds he clearly recognized. Without hesitation he led Alayón directly to a tree whose upper limbs were stripped of bark.

Alayón looked around. Here was a wild and primitive forest, with pine-carpeted mountains plunging steeply down to meet clear green streams lined with thick brush. Locals called the place Ojito de Agua. Ever since Lester Short had left, Alayón had been interviewing mountain people, looking for the best place to begin a new expedition when breeding season began. Ojito de Agua looked like the spot.

Alayón organized an all-Cuban Ivory-bill search team, the first ever. With him were herpetologist Alberto Estrada, two other scientists, a mule driver, four guides—all hunters and miners who knew the mountains like the backs of their weathered hands —and a young photographer named Carlos Peña who had become famous in Cuba as a champion boxer. Their cook was an old woman who kept them strong with rice, beans, and canned meat.

They set out in February 1986, rumbling in a truck to a flat clearing in the lower mountains where they unloaded a huge canvas tent and set up a base camp. Then they divvied up the rest of the gear and food into their *mochilas*, or backpacks. They were fit, well prepared, and optimistic.

The trail to Ojito de Agua seemed to have been made for goats. One part, which they marked as "Three-Rest Mountain," was too steep and rocky for even the agile guides to accomplish in a single climb. For several days the team collected insects and reptiles and searched for Ivory-bills. On the morning of March 13, Estrada caught a brief glimpse of a huge black bird flashing across the path. It might have been a crow, but it struck Estrada as far too big, and he thought he saw white on the wing. Minutes later, several explorers thought they heard an Ivory-bill call far to the south. For the next two days they explored the hills in a state of keen expectation, but found no sign of the great woodpecker. Then, just after breakfast on the morning of March 16, they set out on an old lumber trail that zigzagged along a mountainside. Footing was diffi-

LEARNING ABOUT BIRDS IN CUBA

At this writing, Cuba has about forty professional ornithologists and a much larger number of ornithology students. Classes in the island's natural history begin for all students in fourth grade. Cubans have learned about their birds with very little equipment. The island has little money, and scientists are often restricted by their government from traveling to conferences outside of Cuba.

So Cuban scientists work without batteries, pens, binoculars, paper, thermometers, or gasoline—usually for free. They do it for the love of learning. At Zapata Swamp—a vast ocean of grass like the Everglades—Orestes Martínez, known as "El Chino," has become the world expert on three birds found only there—the Zapata Wren, the Zapata Sparrow, and the Zapata Rail. He started a bird club called "The Three Endemics" to help local children learn about these special birds. "Their fathers and uncles hunted them," he says. "The children want to protect them. That means the birds have hope."

Giraldo Alayón surveys habitat during one of the expeditions when the Ivory-bill was rediscovered in Cuba in the mid-1980s

cult, and the men frequently stumbled. By nine o'clock a light fog had reduced visibility and made the rhythmic crunching of their boots seem even louder. Soon a thin mist glistened on the green crowns of the huge old pine trees.

Alayón was alone in the middle of the pack, trudging with his head down, when he heard a crow call. He lifted his head to the right and, as he remembers, "I saw two big crows chase a female Ivory-bill. They were moving fast, from one side of the valley to the other. It was like a flash. Two big black birds, with another big bird ahead of them. But the one in front had a flash of white on the wings. I was frozen—completely paralyzed. And then it was over so fast. I screamed for the others to come back, but it was gone by the time they got there. I stomped my foot and punched my fist in the air and screamed *'Lo ví! Sí! Sí!'* ['I saw it!'] It was one of the biggest moments of my life."

A week later he returned to Havana and immediately called Lester Short in New York. "I saw the Ivory-bill!" he said. "Come back!" Short was there in a matter of days, this time with his wife, ornithologist Jennifer Horne, as well as sound technician George Reynard. A well-equipped international team explored the forest for ten days straight, with spectacular success. One male Ivory-bill and at least one female were seen seven different times by six different people. The birds streaked across valleys and through trees like black-and-white comets, electrifying anyone who caught a glimpse.

Word of the rediscovery crackled around the island. On their way down the mountain, the searchers were met by a Cuban television crew coming up by mule to interview them. By the time they got back to Havana, even their hotel maids knew. Meetings were arranged with important officials who took notes as Alayón and Short made recommendations much like those of Tanner earlier: no cutting of trees within three and a half miles of the Ivory-bill site; no one allowed in the area except for scientists and wildlife managers; girdling of trees to provide more food. This time Cuban authorities took their advice and closed the area within a week.

Back in the United States, Lester Short told his story to reporters from *People* magazine and *The New York Times*, among many other publications. Privately, he worried about the birds. Though it had been breeding season, they hadn't seemed attached to any one place. Rather than calling to defend nesting territory, they had flown randomly around, acting like the last frantic survivors of a doomed population. "They seemed very wary," Short recalled later. "They were like a hunted animal; they'd just disappear like the mist in front of you. You couldn't even chase them. They should have been on eggs by March, going to a regular site, but there was none of that. I thought maybe we were seeing first-year birds, maybe brother and sister . . . I felt deep in my heart there might not be many more than these two or three."

A year later, in 1987, Giraldo Alayón got one more look at an Ivory-bill. He was again at Ojito de Agua with an all-Cuban crew including his new bride, Aimé Posada, also a biologist from Alayón's hometown of San Antonio. The Ivory-bill expedition was their honeymoon. Their wedding reception had turned into a sort of planning session for the expedition until Aimé had shouted at the biologists, "Hey, this is my wedding day! Stop talking about birds!"

On March 16, the anniversary of the day he had seen the Ivory-bill the preceding year, Alayón awoke with a premonition that he would see it again. He turned to Aimé and whispered, "Today's the day." She didn't stir. He pulled on his boots and went outside to fix *café con leche* for the crew. As the thick brew bubbled, he found himself thinking that maybe he should be paying more attention to crows. Maybe they competed with Ivory-bills for the grubs beneath the bark of the trees. If that was so, crows could be a key to finding the woodpeckers. Shortly after noon, he thought he heard an Ivory-bill call, a single sharp note sounding in the far distance. He couldn't be sure. The crew worked into the blazing heat of the afternoon, then broke for a lunch of sardines, crackers, and juice. Late in the afternoon they relaxed in the camp with a favorite activity: listening to taxidermist Eduardo Solana tell them ghost stories.

At about four-thirty, Giraldo and Aimé hiked back to the spot where Giraldo had first seen the Ivory-bill the year before. It was a good place to find crows. The couple picked their way along the narrow ridge overlooking the Yarey River until Giraldo halted. He turned around to face Aimé and, pointing toward the river, said, "This is the place where I saw the female Ivory-bill the first time." At that very moment three black birds appeared, flying from right to left: a female Ivory-bill being chased by two crows. It was an exact reenactment of what happened on the very same day the year before. The three birds flapped high over the valley, winging back in the direction of the camp until they disappeared. Once again Giraldo was too stunned to reach for the camera that was dangling around his neck. But Aimé was gleeful. "The white patches just shone in the sun," she remembers. "It was so big and pretty." Aimé raced off down the trail to tell the others while Giraldo remained behind in case the Ivory-bill reappeared.

By the time the rest of the team had assembled at the spot it was almost dark. Eduardo Solana said he had seen the Ivory-bill, too, when it flew over the campsite. Chatting excitedly, the team made plans about what they were going to do when they saw it the next day, as they were sure they would. But they didn't see it the next day or the day after that. Though they searched with all their knowledge, strength, and imagination, they never saw it again. And though explorers have tried to find the bird nearly every year since, the sightings of Giraldo, Aimé, and Solana are probably the last anyone in Cuba has seen of the *Carpintero real*. Aimé Posada remains the only Cuban woman ever known to have seen it.

"All the four times I have seen it, I have seen it on March 16," muses Giraldo Alayón in his study. "I think that day has some magic." Alayón himself has led over a dozen expeditions since he last saw the Ivory-bill, all without success. As forests have collapsed throughout the world, finding the Ivory-bill in Cuba has become one of the great quests left in ornithology, like searching for the Fountain of Youth or El

A deserted Ivory-bill roost tree found in eastern Cuba

Dorado. When Alayón is asked, in his small, tidy home filled with bookshelves lined with vials of spider specimens, whether he thinks the Ivory-bill is extinct, he taps on his desk and then answers with the hopeful tone that some U.S. scientists adopt when asked the same question. "Is the bird extinct? . . . Well, no one knows, of course, but if I had to bet, I would say no. No, this bird is still out there somewhere. It is an astonishing bird. It is a soul that links the love of nature and the love of the great forest that was its home. It is still alive. And we will find it."

David Luneau (front) and biologist Richard Hines continue the search for the Ivory-bill in 2003

CHAPTER FOURTEEN
RETURN OF THE GHOST BIRD?

Without [hope], all we can do is eat and drink the last of our resources
as we watch our planet slowly die. Instead, let us have faith in ourselves,
in our intellect, in our staunch spirit.

—Anthropologist Jane Goodall,

who has lived among chimpanzees for more than forty years in Tanzania, Africa

Louisiana, 1986–2002

ANY STUDENT WHO PASSED THROUGH THE OFFICE DOOR OF PROFESSOR JAMES TANNER at the University of Tennessee was brought up short by a sign on his desk. Hand-carved into a block of wood, the message was positioned face out so that a visitor couldn't avoid it. The sign said "STUDY NATURE, NOT BOOKS."

Tanner didn't mean to show disrespect for books. Throughout his long life he had learned a great deal from reading. He was simply trying to pass on a personal truth, one that he had discovered in the low ridges of New York State as a boy. It was a truth that had guided him as a young man as he worked in the last swamp forests of the South, and one that still seemed as good as gold as he helped graduate students with their research in the forests of the Great Smoky Mountains: books helped, but if you wanted to understand nature, you learned your *real* lessons outdoors, watching and listening, noticing and puzzling, and inhaling the fragrance of living things.

Jim Tanner became a distinguished professor, founding the Graduate Program in Ecology at the University of Tennessee. And even as a white-haired old man he was still able to outwalk his graduate students, leaving them gasping and bent over as he strode through the hills.

Still, like a professional athlete, he was always best known for work that he did in the early years of his life. As he sometimes told people, "I am the world expert on an extinct bird." Being the world expert on the Ivory-billed Woodpecker was a little like being a world expert on UFOs or the Loch Ness monster. The job made Tanner the lifetime custodian of rumors, of flashes, of questionable sightings.

In his office, he kept a list of the most believable Ivory-bill sightings. In 1949 there was a report that a pair had survived in the cutover rubble of the Singer Tract. But no one could prove it. The next year a pair was reportedly seen near the Apalachicola River in Florida. There was no evidence. In 1952 there was a report of a sighting twenty miles south of Tallahassee, and in 1954 several more reports from Florida, and on and on—a new report every few years. Tanner put the past behind him and pursued fresh interests, but always the Ivory-bill beckoned. Sometimes he went to track down a rumor himself, just as in the old days, but there was never a clear photograph, never a tape recording, never a moving picture. Tanner thought most of the observers

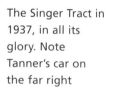

The Singer Tract in 1937, in all its glory. Note Tanner's car on the far right

had really seen Pileated Woodpeckers. He thought the habitat the Ivory-bill needed was gone, that the great bird had truly disappeared from the United States. He tried to gain permission to search for the bird in Cuba, but he couldn't get a visa during the Cold War years.

Tanner returned to the Singer Tract one last time in 1986, after an absence of forty-five years. Now it was called the Tensas River National Wildlife Refuge, and Tanner was invited back to tell the refuge managers about the forest that had been there before. One morning they all took a walk around Little Bear Lake, in the heart of what used to be Ivory-bill country. Passing by the massive stumps of cypress trees cut long ago, Tanner remembered that those very trees had once reminded him of "columns of a Greek temple." His youthful companions noticed that he seemed "pensive," and that he didn't say much. When they asked him how things had changed, he glanced around and said, "There is more sky, smaller trees, more trunks, and more saplings."

There were other changes, of course. The Ivory-bills were missing, as were panthers, wolves, and other creatures Jim Tanner had once known. Even though the Ten-

The same spot, forty-five years later, had become a soybean field

Fifth-grade students take notes on the environment at the Tensas River National Wildlife Refuge in the heart of the old Singer Tract

sas refuge was supposed to cover fifty thousand acres, in fact it covered much less. Bulldozers were still crushing trees to clear land for soybean fields on the very day Tanner arrived.

Tanner stayed in the area for about a week. Just before he left, he admitted that he had been depressed at first when he compared what he saw to his memory of the Singer Tract. But that couldn't keep a sense of optimism from welling up in him. "I'm tickled about the refuge," he told his dinner companions. "It is not as big as I'd like, but it's off to a good start." He hoped the trees remaining along the snaking Tensas River could be left alone to grow in peace. "Every kind of timber type grew in the Singer Tract," he said. "These trees do grow fast, and if you come back in forty years you will be amazed."

"SOMETHING I HAD NEVER SEEN BEFORE"

James Tanner died of a brain tumor in 1991, at the age of seventy-six. After his death, the Ivory-bill rumors and reports that he had fielded for so long went to Louisiana State University, the nearest university to the Singer Tract and the home of LSU's Museum of Natural Science. Since 1979, the museum's curator of ornithology has been Dr. James Van Remsen (known by everyone as "Van"). Most years, Van has gotten about ten reports of Ivory-bills. He has answered them politely, encouraging the caller to send him a photo or a video. Like Tanner, Van has assumed that most of the callers have really seen Pileated Woodpeckers.

Then came April 1, 1999. Early that morning a twenty-year-old LSU forestry student named David Kulivan climbed into his camouflage clothing, grabbed his shot-gun, and drove off to hunt turkey. He chose the Pearl River Wildlife Management Area, a huge, tea-colored swamp forest about an hour from New Orleans. Early that morning, he was sitting quietly against a tree and cradling his shotgun when, he said, two Ivory-billed Woodpeckers landed on a tree nearby. One was a male, the other a female. He said he watched them closely for more than ten minutes and saw all the markings that distinguish an Ivory-bill from a Pileated—the white on the lower wings, the big white bills, the curve of the crests. At one point the birds were no more than thirty feet from where he was sitting. He had a camera, but it was zipped inside his jacket. He decided it would be better to remain still and keep his eye on the birds than to risk scaring them off by removing the camera and snapping the shutter. He later told a reporter, "I knew as soon as I saw them it was something I had never seen before."

Kulivan debated with himself whether or not he should report his finding. On one hand, of course the birding world would want to know. But on the other hand, wouldn't people think he was crazy, or making a story up to attract attention? It didn't help that it had happened on April Fool's Day. Many people before him had re-ported seeing Ivory-bills only to be hooted down by the experts. Did he need that? He decided to tell his wildlife professor, Dr. Vernon Wright. Predictably, Dr. Wright grilled him with hard questions, but Kulivan had all the details right, right down to which way the crests on the heads of a male and female curved.

Dr. Wright sent Kulivan to talk to Van, who in turn put him before a panel of very skeptical experts. No one could crack his story. Van thought it was the best Ivory-bill report he had heard in thirty years. "Kulivan either saw a pair of Ivory-billed Woodpeckers," he said, "or he saw Pileateds and for some reason went nuts . . . He passed with flying colors."

Kulivan's report was kept quiet for nearly a year while all logging in the refuge was suspended and state officials searched for Ivory-bills on foot and from the air. But in January 2000, a Jackson, Mississippi, newspaper broke the story, and overnight, bird-watchers from all over the world flocked to Louisiana. Birders filled up local mo-tels and, flipping out credit cards, emptied the stores of film, batteries, cassette tapes, compasses, insect repellent, sunscreen, and snake boots. Then they waded into the dark waters of the Pearl River. Some played the old Cornell recording on their tape recorders, confusing each other. Some searched in teams, spreading out and communicating by cell phone. One team maintained steady cell-phone contact with a Florida woman who described herself as an "animal communicator." She said she was tuned in to the spirits of woodpeckers. In the end, even her clients sloshed out with soaked trousers and no images or recordings of Ivory-bills.

Van's LSU office became the nerve center of this international sensation. His phone was flooded with reports of Ivory-bill sightings from fifteen states and even Canada—cold, snowy places far from where Ivory-billed Woodpeckers had ever been. Van knew that the logging would soon resume, but he worried. What if the Pearl really *was* the last home for the species? What if they really were out there? Then one day Van got a call from Anthony Cataldo, an executive representing Zeiss Sports Optics, a binocular manufacturer, volunteering to finance a search for the Ivory-bill at the Pearl. Cataldo wanted Van to put together an all-star team of bird experts from around the world for a thirty-day search. Van chose six searchers—two specialists at finding birds in difficult places, three woodpecker experts, and a computer scientist who knew the Pearl River in detail. They rushed to Louisiana, for the world of birding held no greater prize than the rediscovery of the Ivory-billed Woodpecker.

Sixty-six years after Allen, Kellogg, Sutton, and Tanner had recorded the Ivory-bill's voice at Camp Ephilus, Cornell University returned to try again. This time technicians from Cornell's Macaulay Library of Natural Sounds placed twelve microphones at equal distances throughout the swamp. Unlike the bulky old sound mirror that Jim Tanner had to place practically in a bird's nest, these were lightweight computerized microphones called acoustic recording units that detected even the tiniest sounds over great distances and stayed on twenty-four hours a day. Without doubt, the Zeiss search would be the best-equipped, best-planned, and best-financed expedition to search for Ivory-bills since the Cornell sound team's mission of 1935.

Early in January 2002, the six searchers moved into a bunkhouse near Slidell, Louisiana, and began preparations for their mission. Then, for the next thirty days, they sloshed through the thirty-five-thousand-acre swamp and also explored a neighboring area almost as large. They hunted in pairs, swatting away the webs of enormous Banana Spiders as they walked. They were often chest-high in water as they waded across sloughs and creeks. When the water got too deep, they hunted in boats. "Soaking wet" became their normal condition.

Sometimes they came upon tantalizing signs. Broad sheets of bark dangled in loose strips from the high reaches of several trees. They found Ivory-bill-sized cavities dug out of several others. But by far the most dramatic event of all happened on the eleventh day of the search. On the morning of January 27, four of the searchers heard two loud, ringing cracks echo through the swamp, one right after the other. *Ba-DAM!* Then it happened again. *Ba-DAM!* And again. The Cornell microphones picked them up, too. Could this have been the signature double rap of the Ivory-bill? The searchers clicked their hand-held global positioning system units to fix their locations and charged off in the direction of the sound, but the water became too deep. They never heard the sounds again.

After a month, the searchers waded out, cleaned the muck off their gear, and faced the world's cameras and microphones. Foreign reporters participated in a global press conference through a satellite hookup. One of the scientists began by reading a statement the six team members had written together. It said: "We have no proof for the presence of the bird in the area, but think it might be there. In view of the good habitat . . . we recommend more searches in the area." Weeks later, the Cornell Lab of Ornithology reported that computer analysis of the cracking sounds heard on the eleventh day showed that they were made not by woodpecker bills but by rifles.

"WHAT ABOUT THE MITES?"

So the Lord God bird remained a ghost. And as these words are written, it still is. But no one seems to want to give up on it. The bird may be extinct, but our connection to it isn't. Each year, more and more people search for the Ivory-bill in the United States and Cuba, using microphones and cameras that get ever stronger and more sensitive. The silent cassette tapes and empty picture frames people bring back just seem to make them more determined.

Whether anyone finds it again or not, the Ivory-billed Woodpecker may turn out to be the most important bird ever to have lived in the United States. It may be even more important than the Bald Eagle, our national symbol.

Why? Consider just some of the gifts the Lord God bird has given us:

- The Cornell sound expedition of 1935, inspired by the Ivory-bill, gave us the sounds of nearly one hundred other birds. Popular records, cassettes, and CDs of their voices helped make bird-watching popular. Cornell went on to develop techniques which have improved our ability to hear and understand the sounds that birds make.
- The Ivory-bill motivated Doc Allen and others to pioneer ways of providing good clear images and recordings of birds, so that it was less necessary to "collect" study specimens by killing them.
- Jim Tanner's three-year-long study of the Ivory-billed Woodpecker for the Audubon Society was the first detailed study of a bird species that included a conservation plan. It later provided the basis for the first book in an important series of Audubon rare bird studies.
- Richard Pough, the man John Baker sent to the Singer Tract to find the last Ivory-bill, went on to help start the Nature Conservancy, which has worked to save nearly 100 million acres of habitat for threatened species throughout the world.
- The mere report that an Ivory-bill had been heard in South Carolina in the 1970s caused the state to protect ten thousand acres of river swamp forest from being cut. This led to the creation of the Congaree Swamp National Monument, America's biggest park of old river trees—over twenty-two thousand acres.
- Hundreds of thousands of acres in eastern Cuba have been saved for the Ivory-bill, and Cuban schoolchildren are learning more about nature because of the famous woodpecker that was—or is—on their island.

The Ivory-bill's story challenges us to understand creatures on their own terms. Can we get smart enough fast enough to save what remains of our biological heritage? Can we learn to understand and protect creatures that we can't own, pet, walk, or even feed? Can we learn to respect things that might seem ugly, small, and unimportant, simply because we share an experience as living creatures?

One afternoon Dr. James Van Remsen smoothed out the feathers in one of the stiff Ivory-bill specimens in the LSU Museum of Natural Science and said he felt sad that he had never seen the bird alive. They were present during his grandfather's time, even his father's, but barring some kind of miracle, it looked like his chance to see them was gone. It made him angry that humans had knowingly let the bird slip away. He looked at the specimen in his hand. "The challenge isn't so much the Ivory-bill," he said. "What about the *mites* on the Ivory-bill? They weren't doing anybody any good, but what right do we have to make them go extinct?"

Because of the work of Tanner, Allen, Baker, and others, we're lucky to have at least a documented memory of the Ivory-bill and the race to save it. Because they wrote down, photographed, and recorded what they did, these activists and scientists left us a good manual for how to fight skillfully and well. Now it's our turn to do all we can to keep other species from sharing the ghostly fate of the Lord God bird.

Dr. James Van Remsen holds two Ivory-bill specimens

THE COLLAPSING FOREST:
MAPPING THE LOSS OF
IVORY-BILL HABITAT

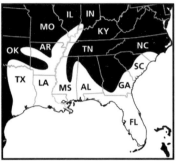

1   Pre-1800

2   1885

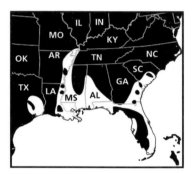

3   1900–1915

$\mathcal{T}$HE DRAMATIC LOSS OF IVORY-BILL HABITAT—FROM A LARGE EXPANSE OF THE SOUTH-eastern United States to a small scrap of land in one swamp forest—can be tracked in this progression of maps, the first six of which are adapted from James Tanner's research in the 1930s.

In Map 1 the white area shows the wide expanse of the Ivory-bill's original distribution, which means that the bird might have been found within this area wherever habitat was suitable.

Maps 2 to 4 show the steady loss of habitat as the great river bottom forests of the American South were cleared away after Reconstruction.

Maps 5 and 6 narrow the focus to the Singer Tract, the Louisiana forest where the Ivory-bill made its last known stand in the United States.

Map 7 shows the site of the successful searches for the Ivory-bill in Cuba in the mid-1980s.

4   1937

7   Mid-1980s

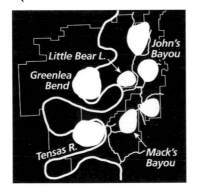

5   1941

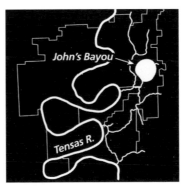

6   1943–1944

A wildlife biologist bands Peregrine Falcon chicks whose nest is in the upper reaches of New Jersey's Walt Whitman Bridge, spanning the Delaware River between New Jersey and Pennsylvania

EPILOGUE

HOPE, HARD WORK, AND A CROW NAMED BETTY

There's one good thing about our species: We like a challenge.
—Edward O. Wilson, Harvard biologist

Planet Earth—the Twenty-first Century and Beyond

ALONG WITH TALES OF EXTINCTION, THE TWENTIETH CENTURY ALSO BROUGHT STORIES of hope and recovery. With each passing decade more people seemed to care about birds. In 1962 Rachel Carson, a biologist from Maine, published *Silent Spring*, warning that pesticides sprayed on plants to kill insects were also poisoning birds and other creatures—including us. Though the chemical and food processing industries ridiculed Carson as a "hysterical woman," she woke up the country. The most harmful pesticides were soon banned. Birds began to recover.

By the 1980s, bird-watching had become a phenomenally popular activity. Millions of birders took to the field with powerful lightweight binoculars hanging from their necks and color field guides jammed into their pockets. Determined to care for the earth and its creatures, more and more high school students chose careers in biology and conservation. With more biologists, better laws, new conservation groups, and more public support, we began to hear stories of species rescued from the brink of extinction.

One such rescue involved a delicate, sand-colored shorebird that has the evolutionary misfortune of laying its speckled eggs in some of the most popular places on

THE ENDANGERED SPECIES ACT OF 1973

By passing and signing the Endangered Species Act of 1973 (known as the ESA), Congress and President Richard Nixon proclaimed that endangered species of plants and animals were valuable for many reasons. They signaled the determination of the United States to save not only the species themselves, but the ecosystems within which they lived. Two lists were made, one for endangered *species (in danger of becoming extinct throughout all or part of their range) and one for* threatened *species (those likely to become endangered without help). Programs were set up to help the listed species.*

Not everyone welcomed this law. Some landowners feared that it would take away their right to use their land as they wished. Some didn't see what the fuss was about— what good were frogs and birds and plants?

*The ESA's first big test came in 1977. Four years before, zoologist David Etnier had discovered a rare little fish known as the Snail Darter (*Percina tanasi*) in the Little Tennessee River. Etnier and his colleagues petitioned to get the darter listed as an endangered species, then filed a lawsuit under the ESA to stop a dam that would have turned the river into a lake and destroyed the darter's habitat. The first judge ruled against them, pointing out that $80 million had already been spent on the dam. But the U.S. Supreme Court overruled him, saying, in Chief Justice Warren Burger's words, "It is clear that Congress intended to halt and reverse the trend toward species extinction whatever the cost."*

earth—beaches. In 1986, the year the Piping Plover (*Charadrius melodus*) was listed under the Endangered Species Act as endangered in part of its range (around the Great Lakes) and threatened in the rest (Atlantic coastal beaches and midwestern rivers and prairie lakes), there were only 2,200 breeding pairs left in the world. Season after season, these little birds struggled to protect their clutches of eggs from beachcombers, dune buggies, dogs, raccoons, gulls, and many other sets of legs and wheels. Things got so bad that some states and Canadian provinces were losing half their plover populations every year.

This meant that government biologists had to create a plan to protect the birds' breeding population. They had no choice but to close some beaches and fence off sections of others during the breeding and nesting season. Howls of protest rose from Cape Cod to Lake Michigan, but the government held firm. Biologists learned year by year what the plovers needed and how to help them.

Today the Piping Plover is recovering, especially in New England. The worldwide population increased by 7.7 percent between 1991 and 1996. While this increase has meant that not everyone can have all parts of a favorite beach at all times during the summer, most people seem willing to share. In some places, "Friends of the Plover" groups have sprung up to protect the plover's breeding habitats. There's still a long way to go, but signs are encouraging.

An even more dramatic success story involves a deadly sky hunter with tapering wings and a distinctive black teardrop below each eye. No hawk is faster—or more acrobatic—than the Peregrine Falcon (*Falco peregrinus*). The Peregrine takes its meals by lifting itself above other birds and then folding in its wings and "stooping" down on them, diving at speeds of up to 200 miles per hour. Often it concludes the chase by neatly shearing off the victim's head in midair with a single stroke of its talons.

In 1970 there were fewer than one hundred Peregrines left in the lower forty-eight states—about 5 percent of their former numbers. They were dying out fast. The main culprit was DDT—a pesticide Rachel Carson targeted in *Silent Spring*. Sprayed on crops to control pests, the poisons in DDT lingered in the tissues of whatever creature ate the crops, such as grasshoppers; then poisoned whatever ate the grasshoppers; and persisted until the poisons reached the top of the food chain. By the time they got to the Peregrine, these poisons made its eggshells so thin that parents crushed their own offspring during incubation. The year after DDT was banned in 1972, the Endangered Species Act was passed and biologists devised a recovery plan for the Peregrines.

As part of this plan, Dr. Tom Cade, a professor of ornithology at Cornell University, requested that falconers—people who legally hunt birds using falcons instead of rifles or arrows—send their Peregrine Falcons to him at the "Peregrine Fund." The idea was to gather the birds together so that they could reproduce in a controlled, protected zoo-like atmosphere before the species died in the wild. The response was immediate: in 1973 twenty new birds were hatched, and the captive population grew steadily year by year.

But where could the new birds be released? Peregrines build their nests high on cliff ledges, where they are commonly raided by the Great Horned Owl, a much bigger bird. There had to be a safer place. Biologists asked themselves: Where are there high ledges with plenty of wild birds flying around for Peregrines to kill and no owls to worry about? Often the answer was right above them: skyscrapers!

Each year, more and more Peregrines perch on the ledges of lofty office buildings, scanning city skylines with their sharp eyes for pigeons and gulls. They raise their

NATURAL HERITAGE INVENTORIES

When poachers shot two Ivory-billed Woodpeckers in Florida in 1924, biologists like Arthur Allen worried that the Ivory-bill had become extinct. They had no way of knowing that the species was still in Louisiana, Cuba, and perhaps elsewhere.

It's easier to know now. In 1974 the state of South Carolina and the Nature Conservancy set up the first State Natural Heritage Inventory. They wanted to keep track of all the state's plant and animal species and types of natural communities—such as forests, marshlands, and prairies.

Workers first researched all the old writings about and museum records of all the state's species—just as Jim Tanner first turned to museum records when he began his Audubon Ivory-bill Fellowship. Then they mapped and recorded data from each old record and put all the information into one central set of files. After that, biologists went out into the field to try to find out if the species was still there. They also ranked how threatened each species was, and how big and healthy each population was. They entered the scientific data into computers.

After a few years the records knitted themselves into a clear picture of the health of South Carolina's biological heritage. Now important habitats for rare species can't be destroyed accidentally.

The idea caught on rapidly. Now there are Heritage Inventories in every state, all the provinces of Canada, and many nations of Central and South America. For more information, log on to www.natureserve.org.

WHAT GOOD IS IT?
WHY SAVE BIODIVERSITY?

Conservationists are often asked: What good is it? Why should we care enough about a bird or a butterfly or a turtle or a snake to go out of our way—or lose money or jobs—to save it? What good is it?

Some answers have to do with the help that creatures give us. Many medicines have come from plants and animals. The blood of armadillos is used in leprosy research. Blood from horseshoe crabs is used to diagnose spinal meningitis in children. Bee venom is used to treat arthritis. It's the same with foods. If we are dependent on only one strain of any crop, it could be wiped out by disease, so we must preserve genetic diversity.

We can't always predict the ways that plants and animals could serve us. During the 1977 Snail Darter controversy, New York senator James Buckley wrote, "What good is a Snail Darter? . . . We simply don't know. What value would they have placed on the cowpox virus before Jenner? Or on a penicillium mold before Fleming? Yet the life of almost every American is different because of those species."

Some species help us measure how healthy the environment is. For instance, honey can be used to detect heavy metal pollution. Parts of certain spiderwort plants turn from blue to pink when exposed to some forms of radiation.

But there are reasons to care about biodiversity besides what living things can do for us. Some spiritual traditions hold that because we can reason, humans are responsible for taking care of life forms that we didn't create but have the power to destroy. By this reasoning, any time we knowingly cause the extinction of a species, we also sacrifice a part of our humanity.

young in nest boxes built by biologists. Now falcons and pigeons engage in spectacular life-and-death aerial chases in city skies high above the heads of gaping shoppers. Hotel guests in upper-floor rooms have been known to fling back their curtains only to see a banquet of severed bird heads arrayed on their window ledges.

On August 20, 1999, after twenty-eight years of never giving up, biologists proudly announced that the Peregrine Falcon had been removed from the U.S. Endangered Species list. Now there were more than 1,700 nesting pairs in the United States, and they were reproducing well both in cities and in their old wild habitats—a triumph of caring and learning to think like a bird!

AND A CROW NAMED BETTY

Most of the birds that we've tried hardest to rescue have been stars and divas. They have been fast, fierce, or beautiful in our eyes, birds that possess qualities we admire. We love the patriotic brow of a Bald Eagle, the aerial acrobatics of a Peregrine Falcon, and, though it's probably too late to rescue them, the dramatic, arrow-like flight of the Ivory-bill. But in addition to these species there are many more that are small, drab, and quiet. Some haven't even been named yet. Many are sinking fast, usually because their habitats are being destroyed too rapidly for them to adapt, to change their genetic habits, just as the Ivory-billed Woodpecker couldn't diversify its diet in time when its forest home was cleared and grubs became scarce. To save breeding populations—enough birds to keep reproducing—for the feathered section of the ark, we're going to have to learn a lot very quickly. Maybe we'll even have to evolve a bit ourselves.

If we can give birds a few thousand more years, they might even learn to help themselves. Consider "Betty." Betty is a crow (*Corvus moneduloides*, to be exact), a member of a species that lives on the island of New Caledonia in the Pacific Ocean. Crows have long been known to be among the smartest of birds. In 2002 researchers studying crow intelligence set up an experiment to see if they would use tools. They placed a small bucket of food inside a tube so slender that Betty and another crow named Abel couldn't climb into it or reach the food with their bills. Researchers gave the crows two pieces of wire to get the food—one crooked and one straight.

Neither crow had any trouble figuring out that you could get the food out of the tube only by using the bent wire to pick up the bucket by its handle. The trouble was, Abel kept stealing the bent wire. Finally, Betty had had enough. She bent the straight wire herself and picked up the bucket. Researchers were amazed—a bird had *made* a tool! "People expect apes to be the pinnacle of intelligence in the animal kingdom because they are our closest relatives," said Alex Kacelnik of Oxford University, who worked on the experiment. "Now a bird is shown to have greater sophistication than many closer relatives of us humans."

Who knows what we humans and birds can learn about each other and about the world we share—if, as we began to do for the Lord God bird, we will just give them time.

IMPORTANT DATES FOR THE PROTECTION OF BIRDS, ESPECIALLY THE IVORY-BILLED WOODPECKER

1607—The government of Bermuda issues a proclamation protecting the cahow and the green turtle—the first species protection acts in the New World.

1731—Mark Catesby provides the first description of the Ivory-bill in his *Natural History of Carolina, Florida and the Bahama Islands*, the first comprehensive English-language study of American plants and animals.

1785—British naturalist Thomas Pennant describes the Ivory-billed woodpecker as "scarce."

1809—Ornithologist Alexander Wilson tries to keep an Ivory-bill in a hotel room in order to paint it, later writes about his experience in a nine-volume work, *American Ornithology*.

1818—Massachusetts bans hunting of larks and robins, the first law protecting non-game (not hunted) species in the United States.

1831—A decade after painting Ivory-bills, John James Audubon writes a detailed description of the species in his *Birds of America*.

1863—The Cuban Ivory-billed Woodpecker is first reported by John Cassin, curator of birds for the Philadelphia Academy of Natural Sciences.

1869—Michigan tries to protect rapidly declining Passenger Pigeons by forbidding guns to be fired within a mile of roosts.

1870s—Much forested land in southern states is released from laws prohibiting sale. Northern and British timber companies begin to clear Ivory-bill habitat to sell the wood.

1877—Florida passes a law forbidding the destruction of the eggs and young of plumed birds. It is widely ignored.

1879—An observer writes of the Ivory-bill: "This bird is not at all abundant, and specimens may be regarded as good additions to one's cabinet."

1890s—Arthur Wayne, W.E.D. Scott, George E. Beyer, and other "collectors" reduce the rapidly diminishing Ivory-bill population in order to sell or exhibit the skins of dead birds.

1893—Johannes Gundlach publishes the first of his two-volume *Ornitologia Cubana*, providing the first detailed description of the Ivory-bill's behavior, appearance, and habitat in Cuba.

1898—After participating briefly in the Spanish-American War, which liberated Cuba from Spain, the United States takes control of much of Cuba's land and economy. Much forested Cuban land is cleared to plant sugarcane, pushing the Ivory-bill deeper into mountainous Cuban habitat.

1901—A course on the protection of certain game birds is required of all Nevada schoolchildren; a non-game-bird protection bill is passed in Florida, which, if it had been enforced, might have protected the Ivory-bill there.

1907—President Theodore Roosevelt, on a hunting trip to northeastern Louisiana, sees three Ivory-bills, calling them the birds "which most interested me" among all he saw.

1910—Responding to pressure from Audubon groups, New York State forbids the sale of wild bird feathers.

1913—The Singer Manufacturing Company purchases nearly 80,000 acres of a swamp forest in Madison Parish, Louisiana, in order to reserve the trees for making sewing machine cabinets. The area becomes known as the Singer Refuge or the Singer Tract.

1914—The Passenger Pigeon becomes extinct; James Tanner is born in Cortland, N.Y.

1918—The last Carolina Parakeet dies in the Cincinnati Zoo.

1924—Arthur and Edna Allen, Cornell University scientists, rediscover the Ivory-bill near the Taylor River, in Florida. The bird had not been reported alive for years.

1932—Louisiana legislator Mason D. Spencer shoots an Ivory-billed Woodpecker in the Singer Tract. Scientists rush to the scene, and six more Ivory-bills are soon found.

1934—A survey shows seven pairs of adult Ivory-bills at the Singer Tract, producing four offspring.

1935—A team of four Cornell University scientists, while on an expedition to record the voices of America's rarest birds, conducts a detailed study of a nesting pair of Ivory-bills at the Singer Tract. They record the species' voice and take still and motion pictures.

1937–1939—Sponsored by the National Audubon Society, Cornell Ph.D. student James Tanner conducts a detailed study of the ecology, biology, and whereabouts of the Ivory-bill. The Singer company begins to sell and lease its forested land to two lumber companies; most goes to the Chicago Mill and Lumber Company, with a large sawmill in nearby Tallulah.

1939—Tanner delivers his final report to the Audubon Society. He estimates there may be twenty-five Ivory-bills alive in the United States, but has found them only at the Singer Tract, where he is able to locate only six Ivory-bills, including just one breeding pair.

1941—With Chicago Mill and Lumber cutting up to 800,000 board feet of lumber a day, the National Audubon Society launches a campaign to stop the cutting and preserve what remains of the Singer Tract as a refuge for Ivory-bills and as a scrap of an ancient forest.

1943—Representatives from the Audubon Society, the U.S. government, and four state governments meet with executives from the Chicago Mill and Lumber Company and the Singer company to discuss preserving a portion of the Singer Tract as a preserve.

1944—Last documented Ivory-bill sightings at the Singer Tract.

1948—U.S. biologists Davis Compton and John Dennis find three Ivory-bills, including a nesting pair, in mountainous eastern Cuba. It is the first report in several years.

1950 (approximately)—The Cuban Ivory-bill is renamed *Campephilus principalis bairdii*, reflecting the belief that the Ivory-bills found in the United States and Cuba are separated populations of the same species rather than two different species.

1951—The Nature Conservancy is established in the United States. It will grow into the world's biggest conservation organization, specializing in saving habitat for imperiled species such as the Ivory-bill and preserving examples of ecosystems such as the swamp forest at the Singer Tract.

1957—U.S. biologist George Lamb discovers thirteen Ivory-bills, including six mated pairs, on Cuban property owned by U.S. corporations; makes conservation recommendations.

1959—The Cuban Revolution freezes contact between Cuban and U.S. scientists and halts progress on Lamb's Ivory-bill conservation plan.

1962—Last documented sighting of Bachman's Warbler and last well-documented sighting of the Eskimo Curlew, both birds that spent part of their life cycles in the United States.

1968—Cuban biologist Orlando Garrido reports Ivory-bills in Cuba for the first time in a decade.

1970—In the United States, students from more than ten thousand schools take part in the first Earth Day, focusing attention on saving species.

1973—The U.S. Endangered Species Act becomes law.

1986—A Cuban expedition led by Giraldo Alayón rediscovers the Ivory-bill in Cuba. One month later, an international team including worldwide woodpecker expert Dr. Lester Short produces several glimpses of a male and a female Ivory-bill.

1987—Giraldo Alayón and Aimé Posada glimpse a female Ivory-bill from a mountainous trail. It is the last certain sighting of the bird.

1999—A hunter delivers a credible report of having seen a male and a female Ivory-bill in the Pearl River Wildlife Management Area, near New Orleans. The report touches off an intensive hunt.

2002—A six-person international team of scientists uses high-tech equipment to search Louisiana's Pearl River Wildlife Management Area and a neighboring swamp for Ivory-bills. They find some signs, but no birds.

GLOSSARY

clutch   A batch of eggs. "Clutch size" means how many eggs are hatched in a single batch. Birds are said to "double clutch" if they lay two batches of eggs in a breeding season. The Ivory-bill had the smallest clutch of any North American woodpecker, two to three eggs.

ecological niche   The sum total of a given organism's relation to its environment, such as where it lives and what it eats. Often the combined activity of different organisms accomplishes a common purpose. The Ivory-billed Woodpecker pried up the bark of dying trees to get at its food. This opened the door for still other creatures to bore into the trees. The trees continued to decompose until eventually they became too weak to stand and fell to the ground, opening holes in the canopy of treetops for sunlight to pour through and illuminate the ground so that new seeds could grow.

ecology   The study of how plants and animals relate to one another and to their physical environment.

ecosystem   A natural community of plants and animals along with the elements of their physical environment, such as soil or a river. No plant or animal can live alone in nature; all living creatures depend on the lives of others and on the environment they share. An ecosystem is a sort of biological neighborhood.

egret   One of several varieties of white heron. The name comes from long plumes called "aigrettes" grown by males during the breeding season.

endemic   A word describing a species that lives only in one place. For example, the Bee Hummingbird, the world's smallest bird, is endemic to Cuba, meaning that it lives only there. The Ivory-billed Woodpecker was not endemic to the United States because there was also a population in Cuba.

evolution   A change in the genes within an entire population of a species by processes such as mutation and natural selection.

extinction   The state of no longer being in existence anywhere.

extirpation   Local extinction. The Ivory-billed Woodpecker probably became extirpated in Louisiana when the Singer Tract was cut, but it did not become extinct, since there was a population still alive in Cuba.

gene   The basic unit of heredity, carried on a chromosome and transmitted from parent to offspring.

grub   The larva of a beetle. The grubs that Ivory bills loved came from three families of the huge order of beetles named Coleoptera.

habitat   A place where a bird or other animal lives, or where we go to find it. It is the place that contains all that a certain animal needs to eat and reproduce.

heron   A tall, long-legged wading bird with a long neck and a long, tapering bill that is used to catch fish and other food. Herons' closest relatives are storks, ibises, and flamingos.

migration   The regular movement of birds between their breeding and nonbreeding areas. This movement is usually seasonal and repeated each year. Some birds, such as the Lesser Golden Plover, fly many thousands of miles in migration each year. Birds migrate for many reasons, including to encounter less competition, to avoid predators, to find more food, to find increased sunlight for feeding and reproduction, and to avoid harsh weather. The Ivory-billed Woodpecker flew long distances to find food, but did not migrate.

natural selection   The process through which forms of life survive and reproduce better than others of their kind by developing traits that allow them to adapt to environmental pressures. For example, over time, each of Darwin's fourteen finch species on the Galápagos Islands evolved from a single founding species through the development of traits—such as different bill shapes—that let them find new sources of food and produce more offspring.

predator   An animal that seizes and eats other animals. The birds most frequently thought of as predators are hawks, eagles, and owls.

preening   Taking care of feathers by fluffing them out and then combing them with the bill. Birds spend a lot of time preening. They preen to make sure that all their feathers are in place, correctly interlocked, and well oiled. Most birds squeeze oil from a gland at the base of their tails onto their bills, which they then use to spread the oil over their feathers. This keeps the feathers from drying out in the sun and keeps birds that live in water warm.

roost   A place where birds sleep, and also the act of sleeping in that place. Some birds, such as blackbirds and starlings, roost together in giant flocks, covering trees or bushes at night. Ivory-bills and other woodpeckers sleep inside cavities, or holes, chiseled into trees.

species   The most basic category into which living things are divided. A species of bird is a kind of bird—such as an Ivory-billed Woodpecker, or a Blue Jay, or an American Robin. But what makes a species a species? One well-respected theory says that a group of birds is a species if the group is reproductively isolated from other groups of birds. This means that members of the group can reproduce only with each other. By this definition, if they tried to reproduce with birds that were not of their species, any young bird that was born could not produce young birds of its own. The question "What makes a species a species?" is still hotly debated among biologists. In other words, it is evolving.

SOURCES

A Note on Sources

This book was a journey for me in two ways. First, it let me write on things I've been thinking about for more than thirty years as an environmentalist and conservationist. I've long been fascinated by the Ivory-billed Woodpecker. I went looking for it myself in the Big Thicket Swamp in Texas in 1980—it was so hot that day I had to carry my dog out. Alas, there were no Ivory-bills, or if there were, they kept out of sight. Second, it was an actual journey in that I hit the road. In a year's time, this book took me to Louisiana, Mississippi, Tennessee, Massachusetts, New York, and Cuba. Often, my most important sources were the people I met and interviewed during this journey.

Research in Cuba was especially exciting. Scouring the island, I found most of the people who had most recently seen the Ivory-bill. I met artists, biologists, stamp collectors, foresters, museum curators, and guides who knew the Ivory-bill in their own ways. Several Cuban educators told me that their students are hungry to learn more about birds, but that poverty forces them to study without binoculars, field guides, drawing paper, even pens and pencils. So, along with several colleagues, I helped start a fund to buy and deliver the supplies they need. For more information on how you can help the Birders' Exchange Cuba Initiative program, see www.americanbirding.org/bex.

General Sources: Books and Magazines

Several books and magazines were more important to my research than all the others:

James T. Tanner, *The Ivory-billed Woodpecker*, Audubon Society Research Report No. 1

(New York: Dover Press, 1942). It's the bible for the Ivory-bill. I first read this book in the 1970s, when I was just beginning my own career as a conservationist. It remains the best study of a single species I've ever read.

Peter Matthiessen, *Wildlife in America* (New York: Viking, 1959). This book gives a detailed snapshot of endangered species in the United States nearly a half century ago.

Christopher Cokinos, *Hope Is the Thing with Feathers* (New York: Warner Books, 2000). Having read Tanner's book about the Ivory-bill, I thought I knew the story of its decline. But Christopher Cokinos broke new ground. His wonderful book—about the disappearance of six American bird species—taught me more and made me want to know much more about the Ivory-bill in the United States and in Cuba. And he left a trail of sources behind that I could research.

David Allen Sibley, ill., *The Sibley Guide to Bird Life and Behavior* (New York: Knopf, 2001). What a treasure! I constantly turned to this beautiful book when I wanted to know something about why birds act as they do.

The Auk. For more than one hundred years, *The Auk*, a quarterly journal of the American Ornithologists' Union, has published original reports on the biology of birds. Tanner, Wayne, Allen, Brewster, Chapman, and other figures in this book published articles in *The Auk*, and, with the help of librarians at Bowdoin College in Maine, I turned to it again and again.

Frank Graham, Jr., *The Audubon Ark: A History of the National Audubon Society* (New York: Knopf, 1990). By far the best single source of information I found on the history of the Audubon Society and the Plume War.

Barbara and Richard Mearns, *The Bird Collectors* (San Diego: Academic Press, 1998). Here is a gold mine of information on collectors and collecting, covering everything from Ward's Natural Science Establishment to a ranked list of the greatest collections of bird specimens in the world.

Fortunately, the Ivory-bill was so striking in appearance that many of the people who saw it wrote something about it. Here are the more important sources by chapter.

Prologue. The Hostage

Alexander Wilson's famous account of trying to keep an Ivory-bill in his hotel room appears in his *American Ornithology* as part of a long description of the Ivory-billed Woodpecker. I used the Brewer edition (Boston, 1840), pp. 272–79. All quotes attributed to Wilson in "The Hostage" are from this book, including the opening quote on p. 7. For more information about Wilson's life and times, I turned especially to Robert Cantwell, *Alexander Wilson: Naturalist and Pioneer, a Biography* (Philadelphia: Lippincott, 1961). The quote from Charles Leslie in the sidebar on p. 9 is from Cantwell, p. 144.

Chapter One. Specimen 60803

I visited the Louisiana State University Museum of Natural Science in January 2002. Dr. James Van Remsen showed me Ivory-bill specimens and patiently answered questions about the species' life history. Much in this chapter is based on this interview.

"Weight-Saving Features" (sidebar, p. 14): I especially used Sibley and Dr. Ernst Mayr, *What Evolution Is* (New York: Basic Books, 2001), in order to understand more about how birds evolved and why they are formed as they are and behave as they do.

A good discussion of Darwin's finches (sidebar, p. 15) is found in Roger F. Pasquier, *Watching Birds: An Introduction to Ornithology* (Boston: Houghton Mifflin, 1977), pp. 24–27.

To learn about the structure and behavior of woodpeckers, I consulted Dr. Lester L. Short, *Woodpeckers of the World* (Greenville, Del.: Weidner & Sons/Delaware Museum of Natural History, 1982), and T. Gilbert Pearson, "Woodpeckers, Friends of Our Forests," *National Geographic*, vol. 63, no. 4 (April 1933).

Almost all material on George E. Beyer, including the quote on p. 18 from Beyer to W. D. Rogers, came from materials in a file under Beyer's name in the Special Collections Division of the Tulane University Library. The newspaper article about Beyer's experiment with rattlesnake venom is from *The Daily Picayune* (New Orleans) of September 2, 1905. Quotes on p. 18 in which Beyer describes collecting Ivory-bills are from his article "The Ivory-billed Woodpecker in Louisiana," in *The Auk*, vol. 17, no. 2 (April 1900).

Chapter Two. Audubon on the Ivory-billed Frontier

The introductory quote ("He neglects his material interests") appeared in an article by Michael Harwood and Mary Durant, "In Search of the Real Mr. Audubon," in *Audubon Magazine*, vol. 87, no. 3 (May 1985), p. 63. John James Audubon's descriptions of the Ivory-billed Woodpecker, its voice, its habitat and behavior, and the quotes about the killing of Ivory-bills by Indians and settlers appear in Audubon's *The Birds of America* (New York: J. J. Audubon; Philadelphia: J. B. Chevalier, 1840–44). Besides Audubon's great paintings, one can find nearly five hundred fascinating descriptions of the birds Audubon encountered. For biographical information about Audubon, I turned to several books, especially Shirley Streshinsky, *Audubon: Life and Art in the American Wilderness* (New York: Villard Books, 1993), Alice Ford, *John James Audubon* (Norman: University of Oklahoma Press, 1964), and Alexander B. Adams, *John James Audubon: A Biography* (New York: G. P. Putnam's Sons, 1966).

Audubon kept a journal of his daily observations during his 1820–1821 voyage down the Ohio and Mississippi rivers with Joseph Mason and also wrote about a few months they spent together in New Orleans. It is here that I found Audubon's quotes about Mason and his description of shooting an Ivory-billed Woodpecker. I used *Journal of John James Audubon, 1820–1821* (Boston: Club of Odd Volumes, 1929).

Also, there have been two good books of fiction about Joseph Mason for young readers.

While I couldn't quote from them in this nonfiction book, they provided a good sense of Mason's amazing adventures with Audubon. They are Barbara Brenner, *On the Frontier with Mr. Audubon* (Honesdale, Pa.: Boyds Mills Press; reprint edition, 1997), and Charlie May Simon, *Joe Mason: Apprentice to Audubon* (New York: E. P. Dutton, 1946).

The quotes on p. 24 from Mark Catesby come from a volume that is usually considered to be the first American natural history. Catesby was a British gentleman trained in botany and natural history. A century after the British finally established colonies in the New World, he hungered to see the region's fabled plants and animals. After his sister Elizabeth moved to Williamsburg, Virginia, Catesby used her home as a base and spent ten years exploring Britain's southern colonies in America between 1712 and 1725. He collected specimens, took careful notes, and painted watercolors. Then he returned to London and spent twenty years writing up his findings. When he was ready, he dedicated his two-volume work to Queen Caroline and gave it a title that can hardly be said in one breath: *The Natural History of Carolina, Florida and the Bahama Islands: Containing the Figures of Birds, Beasts, Fishes, Serpents, Insects and Plants . . . To which are added, Observations on the Air, Soil, and Waters: With Remarks upon Agriculture, Grain, Pulse, Roots, &c.* I found Catesby's work on microfilm at the University of Southern Maine.

Chapter Three. "The Road to Wealth Leads Through the South"

A good book for learning about the southern lumber boom is historian C. Vann Woodward's *Origins of the New South: 1877–1913* (Baton Rouge: Louisiana State University Press, 1971). Chauncy Depew's quote at the beginning of the chapter is from p. 115 of this book. Woodward describes the feverish sale of southern forested land at the end of Reconstruction and the great desire of Northerners to get at it. The quotes on p. 33 from "a Chattanooga, Tennessee, newspaper" and from a "government forestry expert" are also from Woodward, both on p. 118. Mary E. Tebo shared additional insights through her excellent, as yet unpublished master's study, conducted for Florida State University, entitled "The Southeastern Piney Woods: Describers, Destroyers, Survivors."

To learn about the clearing of northern forests, I turned to Matthiessen, *Wildlife in America*, and to several Web sites, especially Andy Hiltz, "Logging the Virgin Forests of West Virginia" (www.patc.net/history/archive/virgfst.html). Cotton Mather's quote on p. 30 came from Matthiessen, p. 56, and Daniel Boone's remark to Audubon on p. 31 is also from Matthiessen, p. 112. I found Thomas Nuttall's opinion on p. 33 that the Ivory-bill was restricted to the Gulf States and Lower Mississippi Valley in his *A Popular History of the Ornithology of Eastern North America* (Boston: Little, Brown, 1896), p. 443. I turned to my own article "A Stand for the Ages" for information about the history and destruction of the virgin forests in the upper Connecticut River valley in New Hampshire. Detailing how the last stand of virgin spruce in New Hampshire was saved by a visionary forester, it appears in *Nature Conservancy* magazine, vol. 38, no. 5 (September 1988).

Chapter Four. Two Collectors

James Tanner's introductory quote on p. 35 appears on p. 19 of his book *The Ivory-billed Woodpecker*.

The description of Charleston on p. 35 ("a city of . . . vacant houses"), attributed to a "writer," appears in Joy Hakim's *A History of Us* (New York: Oxford University Press, 1994), vol. 7, p. 13.

Several articles in *The Auk* were especially helpful in this chapter. In Arthur T. Wayne's "Notes on the Birds of the Wacissa and Aucilla River Regions of Florida," *The Auk*, vol. 12 (1895), pp. 364–67, Wayne—in the quote appearing on p. 43—blames "the crackers" for the decline of the Ivory-bill along a Florida river. William Brewster and Frank M. Chapman describe a grand trip down the Suwannee River, during which they shot an Ivory-bill, in "Notes on the Birds of the Lower Suwannee River," *The Auk*, vol. 7, no. 2 (April 1891), pp. 125–38.

Henry Henshaw's description of the equipment he took with him on a collecting expedition (sidebar, "Market Hunters," on p. 40) appears in Mearns, *The Bird Collectors*, p. 56.

There is a splendid memorial biography of William Brewster by Henry Wetherbee Henshaw in *The Auk*, vol. 37, no. 1 (January 1920), pp. 1–32. *The Auk* also published an equally impressive memorial tribute to Arthur T. Wayne by Alexander Sprunt, Jr., in vol. 48, no. 1 (January 1931), pp. 1–16. Here I found the quote about Wayne appearing on p. 37.

Information about Wayne's collecting activities in Florida in 1892–94, including his letters to Brewster, are found in the Special Collections Department of the Ernest Mayr Library of the Museum of Comparative Zoology, Harvard University, in files under "William Brewster" and "Ivory-billed Woodpecker." There you will find Wayne's quotes on pp. 41 and 41–42 and the price list on p. 42. For information about the Charleston Museum and Wayne's activities on its behalf I consulted Albert E. Sanders and William D. Anderson, Jr., *Natural History Investigations in South Carolina: From Colonial Times to the Present* (Charleston: University of South Carolina Press, 1999). The quote from Elliott Coues on p. 43 comes from Mearns, *The Bird Collectors*, p. 19, as does the quote on p. 44 that begins "Collecting provided a convenient and socially acceptable excuse," at p. 21. *The Bird Collectors* contains material on the technique of taxidermy, on cabinet collectors, market hunters, Ward's Natural Science Establishment, the world ranking by number of specimens of Brewster's collection, and a little about Brewster himself.

The Henry Augustus Ward Papers, documenting the life and times of the founder of Ward's Natural Science Establishment, are in the Rare Books, Special Collections, and Preservation department of the Rush Rhees Library of the University of Rochester, New York. Consult www.lib.rochester.edu/rbk/haward.stm.

I discovered more about Wayne through interviews with Dr. Will Post and Dr. Albert E. Sanders of the Charleston Museum.

Chapter Five. The Plume War

Graham's *The Audubon Ark* tells of Frank Chapman's stroll in New York City counting birds on women's hats. Graham also presents the story of Harriet Hemenway, including, at p. 15, the quote from her cousin Minna Hall (pp. 49–50). Graham also writes of the murder of Guy Bradley and the capture of Arthur Lambert and provides much information about the legal protection for birds brought about by the Audubon movement. The quote on p. 49 that begins "Here and there in the mud" appears in Graham at p. 14. I found Chapman's quote in the sidebar on p. 49, "a new kind of Christmas side hunt," in Graham at p. 38. Matthiessen's *Wildlife in America* also reports the Chapman stroll and Bradley's murder and presents a valuable chronology of important laws to protect U.S. wildlife up to 1959.

A thrilling account of Guy Bradley's boyhood plume-collecting trip for "the Frenchman" along the tip of Florida is Charles William Pierce's "The Cruise of the *Bonton*," in *Tequesta*, published by the Historical Association of Southern Florida, vol. 22 (1962), pp. 3–62.

Plume trade statistics come from Paul R. Ehrlich, David S. Dobkin, and Darryl Wheye, "Plume Trade" (www.Stanfordalumni.org/birdsite/text/essays/Plume_Trade.html).

Roger Tory Peterson's boyhood birding experiences, including those with the Bronx County Bird Club, are found in Graham, pp. 129–35, and in Peterson's interview with the National Wildlife Federation, found at www.nwf.org/internationalwildlife/peterson.html, which contains the quotes on p. 54.

Arthur "Doc" Allen's trip with his wife, Edna, to Florida, where they saw the Ivory-bill in 1924, is reported in his article "Recent Observations on the Ivory-billed Woodpecker," in *The Auk*, vol. 54 (April 1937), pp. 164–84. All quoted newspaper accounts of the trip and correspondence with Morgan Tindall are found in the Arthur Allen collection at Cornell University's Rare and Manuscript Collections Division (file number 21-18-1255, Box 2). Here, too, in an Associated Press story dated July 12, 1924, and headlined RARE BIRD REPORTED IN CENTRAL FLORIDA, I discovered Allen's quote on p. 56 that begins "As long as the state of Florida allows . . ." A personal interview with the Allens' son David C. Allen provided additional information. The story about Allen's experiment with the eagle and the hen on pp. 54–55 came from George Miksch Sutton, *Bird Student* (Austin: University of Texas Press, 1980), p. 201.

Chapter Six. Learning to Think Like a Bird

Learning about James Tanner's boyhood was one of the best parts of researching this book. Much of my information came from his widow, Nancy Tanner. I visited her at the small house in the wooded hills on the outskirts of Knoxville, Tennessee, that the Tanners shared for many years. Mrs. Tanner told me stories and trusted me with valuable materials. After that, we had three telephone interviews and dozens of e-mail exchanges. I also interviewed James's boyhood friend Carl McAllister several times, as well as the Tanners' son David. The Cortland, New York, Free Library maintains a small file on Tanner.

The lines from Emily Dickinson quoted at the opening of this chapter (p. 59) are from her poem 932, written in 1864. A colorful account of Cornell's McGraw Hall is found in George Miksch Sutton, *Bird Student* (Austin: University of Texas Press, 1980), pp. 209–16. The quote in the sidebar on p. 62 about the "Roughing-Out Room" appears in Sutton, p. 213. The quote on p. 65 beginning "the wildest of yells" is in Sutton, p. 210. Tanner's college transcripts, showing the courses he took and the (very good) grades he earned are found in his file at the Cornell University Rare and Manuscript Collections Division, as is information about where he lived and what it was like to be an ornithology student in those years. The account of the Monday night "seminar" came from an interview with Sally Hoyt Spofford.

Information about the organization of the Cornell sound expedition came from the Web site of Cornell's Macaulay Library of Natural Sounds (http://birds.cornell.edu/lns) and from Arthur Allen's files at Cornell. Doc Allen's quote on p. 66 about the new kind of "hunting" expedition is from Allen's article "Hunting with a Microphone the Voices of Vanishing Birds," *National Geographic*, vol. 71, no. 6 (June 1937), p. 697. Allen's description of Tanner as a "handy man" (on p. 67 and again in chapter 8, on p. 82) appears in the same article at p. 699, as well as on the second page of the introduction to the memoir of the expedition (see sources for chapters 7 and 8). Tanner's selection is also described in a newspaper article entitled "Cortland Student at Cornell Chosen to Take Part in Expedition to Study Rare Bird Life," in Tanner's file at Cornell, Box 6 (see sources for chapter 9). Unfortunately, the newspaper is not identified, nor is the article dated.

Chapter Seven. Shooting with a Mike *and*
Chapter Eight. Camp Ephilus

Dr. Boonsong Lekagul (1907–1992), the author of chapter 7's opening quote (p. 69), is revered as the father of Thailand's national park system. He began his connection with wildlife as a hunter, but put away his rifle when he realized many species were being slaughtered. During the 1950s and '60s he campaigned tirelessly for conservation in his war-torn land by writing letters and articles and by hosting a regular radio and television program. Frustrated that Thai prime minister Field Marshal Sarit Thanarat wouldn't believe that Thailand's forests were being destroyed, Dr. Boonsong arranged to take him on a helicopter ride over the ruined Dong Phaya Yen forest. Shortly afterward, Thailand created a law to protect hunted species, and, in 1962, passed its National Park Act. Dr. Boonsong's quote is from Mearns, *The Bird Collectors*.

The memoir of the "Brand–Cornell University–American Museum of Natural History Ornithological Expedition," created by the participants, recounts this remarkable quest. It is a brilliant photographic record and includes an introduction by Doc Allen. Only a few copies of this bound memoir were made for those who went on the trip and a few others who supported the expedition. The only publicly available copy I know of is at the Cornell University Rare and Manuscript Collections Division.

Another rich source of information about the Cornell sound expedition is Arthur Allen's "Recent Observations on the Ivory-billed Woodpecker" (see sources for chapter 5). Here I found the Cornell team's journal entries presented in chapter 8—see especially the quote at p. 81—and the story about the "crawling sawdust," and, at p. 179, the "weak buzzing" quote from Allen that appears on p. 85. Another good source is Allen's "Hunting with a Microphone the Voices of Vanishing Birds," *National Geographic*, vol. 71, no. 6 (June 1937), pp. 697–723. The story of Mason D. Spencer's shooting of an Ivory-bill (p. 70) is told by George Miksch Sutton in his *Birds in the Wilderness* (New York: Macmillan, 1936), including Spencer's quotes, at pp. 190–91. Likewise, Sutton's book provided a firsthand account of the Cornell team's rediscovery of the Ivory-bill on pp. 191–96. Here I found the two quotes from J. J. Kuhn that appear on p. 73. Christopher Cokinos added sharp perspective in his account of the expedition in *Hope Is the Thing with Feathers*. Interviews with Nancy Tanner filled in many details, including the joy that Jim felt in being on the trip.

Emerson's quote opening chapter 8 (p. 79) comes from his address entitled "The Method of Nature," published from "Addresses" in his *Nature: Addresses and Lectures* (Boston: Houghton Mifflin, 1849). Helpful information about the Taensa Indians appears in *The Catholic Encyclopedia*, vol. 14 (New York: Robert Appleton, 1912). Theodore Roosevelt's story of his visit to the Tensas swamp appeared as "In the Louisiana Canebrakes" in *Scribner's Magazine*, vol. 43, no. 1, pp. 47–60.

Information on the purchase of forested land in Madison Parish by Douglas Alexander of the Singer company came from Madison Parish Courthouse land records. Much information on Alexander and the Singer company appears in Don Bissell, *The First Conglomerate: 145 Years of the Singer Sewing Machine Company* (Brunswick, Me.: Audenreed Press, 1999).

An account of one boy's experience of the terrifying black wall of dust that rose on April 8, 1935, is in my book *We Were There, Too! Young People in U.S. History* (New York: Farrar, Straus and Giroux, 2001), at pp. 196–98.

A videocassette of the Cornell team's recording of the Ivory-bill was made by Cornell University. It's amazing . . . for a few ghostly seconds one can hear the great bird and see it move. One can also see Allen and Kellogg and catch a glimpse of Tanner as he stumbles through the mud behind Ike's wagon. Contact Cornell University's Rare and Manuscript Collections Division, Carl A. Kroch Library, Cornell University, Ithaca, NY 14853. The sound recording of the Ivory-bill may be accessed via the Cornell site (http://birds.cornell .edu/ivory/)—click on "Listen to a clip of their recording." It can also be found on Mangoverde World Bird Guide (www.mangoverde.com/birdsound).

Chapter Nine. Wanted: America's Rarest Bird *and*
Chapter Ten. The Last Ivory-bill Forest

The profile of John Baker is drawn from three sources. First, the National Audubon Society's archives, located in Room 328 of the Fifth Avenue and Forty-second Street Branch of the New York Public Library, include Baker's correspondence, filed under "NAS records, section b, John Hopkinton Baker." There I found Baker's quote on p. 89 ("Every plant and animal . . ."). Second, Frank Graham wrote extensively about Baker in *The Audubon Ark*. Finally, Richard C. Pough addressed Baker's "imposing" personality in two personal interviews with me in 2002.

At Cornell, in the Carl A. Kroch Library at the Rare and Manuscript Collections Division, there is an extensive file of James Tanner's correspondence and work. The file, under his name, is identified as no. 2665. It consists of several boxes and is nothing less than a treasure. Here I found most of my information about his activities during his Audubon Research Fellowship, which lasted from 1937 to 1939. Tanner kept a daily journal, but only a few notebook pages from March 1938 survive in his file. However, he did compile detailed reports of his activities a half year at a time, organized chronologically, often in two- or three-day summaries. Most of this material is in Box 1. Here he tells where he went and what he found in his Ivory-bill quest, including his trip down the Altamaha River (pp. 92–93) and his explorations in Florida (pp. 93–95). Here, too, is Tanner's reaction to the cutting of trees at the Singer Tract ("Those woods should be *preserved*," p. 99) and the valentine to his car that appears on p. 99.

But that's not all. Tanner's Cornell file contains penny postcards sent to Arthur Allen, as well as Doc Allen's letter confirming that Tanner is "reliable and trustworthy" (p. 92). Even Tanner's expense reports are fascinating. He did everything he could to save money, including sleeping on the ground and lunching on chocolate bars, which didn't cost much.

Also in Tanner's Cornell file is his paper "The Suwannee River, 1890 and 1973," which tells of his encounter with the men at the Suwannee River campsite (pp. 94–95).

The aims of Tanner's study and how he organized his time are detailed in his book *The Ivory-billed Woodpecker*. Here I found maps of places he visited or read about, and a good description of his research techniques. His Ivory-bill aliases (sidebar, p. 92) are found at p. 101, while comparisons between Ivory-bills and Pileated Woodpeckers (sidebar, p. 93) are at p. 2.

Later in his life, Tanner wrote two long and valuable reminiscences of his days at the Singer Tract. One, entitled "A Forest Alive," appears in the British magazine *Birdwatch*, issue 107 (May 2001), pp. 18–24. This is the basis for most of the descriptions of the Singer forest in the first pages of chapter 10, including the story of Tanner's encounter with a wolf (p. 104), his account of rowing out onto a lake at night (pp. 104–5), of the snakes he and J. J. Kuhn encountered (p. 105), of the awesome falling of giant trees (p. 105), and of his day-end conversations with Kuhn (p. 105). A second Tanner reminiscence, entitled "A Postscript on Ivorybills," appears in *Bird Watcher's Digest* (July–August 2000). Here Tanner described his acquaintance with "Sonny Boy" (pp. 106–9).

Tanner's conclusions about what it would take to save the Ivory-bill are best presented in his book, but they appear first in his 1939 year-end report for the Audubon Society, entitled "Report of the Ivory-billed Woodpecker Fellowship before the National Association of Audubon Societies, October, 1939," found in Box 1 of Tanner's Cornell file. The quote that opens chapter 10, at p. 101 ("The Ivory-bill has frequently been described . . .") is taken from p. 5 of this report. The quote at p. 112 ("less dead wood . . .") is from p. 8. His tribute to the Singer Tract on p. 113 ("the finest stand of virgin swamp forest") is from p. 10. Tanner makes his first ominous reference to the cutting of trees at the Singer Tract in a report entitled "Field Work in December 1937," at p. 4, under the heading "Recent Developments in the Singer Tract."

Chapter Eleven. The Race to Save the Lord God Bird

"The Story of the Chicago Mill and Lumber Company," by John R. Shipley, is an 18-page un-published company history. It was written in 1980 by a Chicago Mill employee and is available at the Washington County Historical Society in Greenville, Mississippi. It provided detailed information about the company's origins and development and logging of the Singer Tract.

Douglas Alexander's attitudes toward flappers are discussed in Don Bissell's *The First Conglomerate* (see sources for chapters 7 and 8).

Insights about portable housing at Singer came from personal interviews with Billy Louis Fought, who lived in such a house, and Tolbert Williams. They also told me about the furious pace of Chicago Mill's logging, as did Gene Laird, in an interview at his home. Further information on Chicago Mill's cutting is found in a letter to Tanner from Louisiana conservation official George H. Buck, dated August 11, 1941, and found in Tanner's Cornell file, Box 1.

Gene Laird's quote ("Those woods were *loud*") on p. 116 came from my interview with Mr. Laird. The "Swamp Date" (pp. 118–20) was lovingly recalled by Nancy Tanner in telephone interviews and e-mail correspondence.

The John Baker collection in the National Audubon Society archives at the New York Public Library (see sources for chapter 9) is huge. Most of this material is available on microfilm. Most valuable is a sub-file labeled "The Singer Tract," within which I found accounts of James Tanner's walk with Sam Alexander (pp. 120–21), Governor Sam Jones's provision of $200,000 to buy land at Singer (p. 122), and a copy of H.R. 9720.

The first meeting between Audubon's Baker and Chicago Mill's Griswold ("Mr. Griswold has just been with me here . . .") on p. 122 is documented in Tanner's Cornell file, Box 1 (letter, Baker to Tanner, March 25, 1942). Tanner's recommendation that Greenlea Bend be saved ("it is the gem of it all") on p. 121 comes from his 9-page typewritten "Report on Trip to the Singer Tract, Louisiana, December 1941," found in Tanner's Cornell files.

Baker's instructions to Richard Pough to slip down to Louisiana (p. 123) and look for Ivory-bills are found in a long "Memorandum to Mr. Pough," in the National Audubon Society's Singer Tract sub-file.

Census data for Madison Parish are found at www.census-online.com/links/LA/Madison.

A good discussion of Executive Order 8802 is found in Ronald Takaki's *A Different Mirror* (Boston: Little, Brown, 1993), in chapter 14.

Chapter Twelve. Visiting with Eternity

The opening quote, on page 125, appears in Matthiessen's *Wildlife in America*, at p. 253.

In 2002 I interviewed Billy Louis Fought and his brother, Robert Fought, about what it was like to grow up on the Singer Tract as it was being logged, and about their time with the late Don Eckelberry. Likewise, Mr. Eckelberry's widow, Virginia, shared information in a telephone interview about her husband's temperament and work. Don Eckelberry described his days with the last female Ivory-bill in a wonderful chapter, "Search for the Rare Ivorybill," in the book *Discovery: Great Moments in the Lives of Outstanding Naturalists*, ed. John K. Terres (Philadelphia and New York: J. B. Lippincott, 1961).

Much firsthand information about German POWs in Louisiana came from two interviews with John Cherbini, who served as a prison guard in Tallulah during World War II. He went to New York City and escorted German prisoners to Louisiana, then supervised their work at a campground outside Tallulah. He was with them as they logged the Singer Tract.

Information on Chicago Mill and Lumber Company's wartime activities, including the manufacture of tea chests for British troops (p. 130) is found in Shipley, "The Story of the Chicago Mill and Lumber Company" (see chapter 11 source notes).

There is a good exhibit about the Afrika Korps soldiers in the Hermione Museum in Tallulah, including a few examples of prisoner carvings. Tolbert Williams and Gene Laird shared personal reminiscences of the POWs and took me to barns prisoners had built, with German names still carved in the doors. Good written materials include James E. Fickle and Donald W. Ellis, "POW's in the Piney Woods," *The Journal of Southern History*, vol. 56, no. 4 (November 1990)—the two quotes on p. 127, "When we Germans hear the word 'forest,'" and "Who does not know these little red stitches," are from p. 702 of this article. I also consulted Matthew J. Schott and Rosalind Foley, *Bayou Stalags: German Prisoners of War in Louisiana* (Lafayette, La.: self-published, 1981), and Joe Danborn, "War Is Swell," *Gambit Weekly* (January 19, 1999). I interviewed Dr. Matthew J. Schott, a former professor of history at the University of Southwestern Louisiana (now the University of Louisiana at Lafayette), and the expert on POWs in his state. His interest began as a boy of eight, when three German POWs were assigned to trim his mother's backyard azalea bushes at a time when his three older brothers were fighting Nazis overseas. His mother gave them Cokes, explaining to Matthew that she hoped that someone would treat his brothers the same way if they were shot down or captured.

The account of the showdown meeting at Chicago Mill and Lumber's office on pp. 128–29 containing the "We are just money grubbers" quote comes from a report by

Audubon's John Baker entitled "For the Confidential Information of the Directors of National Audubon Society, December 15, 1943." It is found in the Singer Tract sub-file in the Audubon archives at the New York Public Library (see sources for chapter 9). In this file I found extensive, illuminating correspondence between Baker and Richard Pough, the man assigned to keep track of the last bird, including the two Pough quotes on p. 129 ("It is sickening to see . . ." and "I watched them cutting . . ."). Gene Laird told me, during an interview, about keeping track of the last Ivory-bill after Mr. Eckelberry had departed. The story appears on pp. 132–33.

Chapter Thirteen. *Carpintero Real*: Between Science and Magic

Dr. James Van Remsen of Louisiana State University patiently explained the shift in taxonomic thinking about the Cuban and U.S. populations of the Ivory-bill.

Orlando H. Garrido and Arturo Kirkconnell's superb *Field Guide to the Birds of Cuba* (Ithaca, N.Y.: Cornell University Press, 2000) reveals much about Cuba's natural history, as did a lecture I attended on May 29, 2002, at Harvard University by Giraldo Alayón.

I visited Cuba three times between 2002 and 2004. Two interviews with Giraldo Alayón at his home in San Antonio de los Baños offered wonderful insights about the expeditions in Cuba and his personal involvement with the Ivory-billed Woodpecker there. One of the conversations also produced this chapter's opening quote, on p. 135. I was also able to interview Giraldo's wife, Aimé Posada, during the second of these two conversations. These talks were followed by several telephone conversations, a visit by Alayón to the United States, and dozens of e-mail exchanges. Quotes attributed to Alayón and Posada throughout chapter 13 came from these conversations and this correspondence. Alayón's recollections were supplemented by interviews with Cuban biologists Carlos Peña, Arturo Kirkconnell, Orlando Garrido, and Xiomara Gálvez Aguilera.

The account on page 141 of Alberto Estrada's glimpse of a big bird that he believed to be an Ivory-bill comes from the article "Of Woodpeckers and Frogs," by Alberto R. Estrada. It appears on pp. 75–87 of *Islands and the Sea: Essays on Herpetological Exploration in the West Indies*, ed. Robert W. Henderson and Robert Powell, *Contributions to Herpetology* 20 (Ithaca, N.Y.: Society for the Study of Amphibians and Reptiles).

By telephone from his home in Kenya, Lester Short shared his memories of tracking the Cuban Ivory-bill. His observation that the Ivory-bills he saw in Cuba seemed "very wary" (p. 143) came from a telephone interview. Dr. Short also wrote two articles in *Natural History* magazine whose titles reflect the mood of the searches. The first is called "Last Chance for the Ivory-bill" (vol. 94, 1985). A year later, Short and his wife, Jennifer Horne, co-authored "The Ivory-bill Still Lives" (vol. 95, 1986).

Any discussion of the Cuban Revolution is controversial, but I admire Christopher P. Baker's even-handed discussion in *Moon Handbooks: Cuba* (Emeryville, Calif.: Avalon Travel Publishing, 1999).

The story in the sidebar on p. 139 about Orlando Garrido's stopping an international tennis match to collect an insect is legendary in Cuba. I heard it from several sources and was finally able to hear Garrido tell it himself in a telephone interview in Havana in March of 2003.

Information in the sidebar "Learning About Birds in Cuba" on p. 141 comes from my discussions with Cuban biologists and from an article, "Getting Things Done in Cuba," by Steve Hendrix in *International Wildlife* magazine (January/February 2000). In this article I found the discussion of Orestes Martínez and his "Three Endemics" club presented in the same sidebar.

George R. Lamb reports his successful 1957 expedition in quest of the Cuban Ivory-bills in *The Ivory-billed Woodpecker in Cuba* (New York: Pan-American Section, International Committee for Bird Preservation, Research Report 1, 1957). John Dennis reports his 1948 quest in "A Last Remnant of Ivory-billed Woodpeckers in Cuba," *The Auk*, vol. 65, no. 4 (October 1948).

Chapter Fourteen. Return of the Ghost Bird?

Jane Goodall's quote at the chapter opening (p. 147) comes from her essay "My Three Reasons for Hope"; the full essay appears on the Web site of the Jane Goodall Institute (www.jane goodall.org/janc/cssay.html).

The story of Jim Tanner's return to the Singer Tract (pp. 149–50) came from interviews and correspondence provided by Nancy Tanner. Most helpful was a newspaper article of March 25, 1986, entitled "Tanner Returns to the Tensas," by staff writer Amy Ouchley of the *Madison Journal*, Tallulah, Louisiana. Tanner's list of Ivory-bill sightings is found in his file at Cornell (see sources for chapter 9).

David Kulivan's purported sighting of the Ivory-bill, reported on pp. 150–51, and the subsequent dragnet for the birds in the Pearl River Wildlife Management Area have been described in hundreds of articles, magazine stories, and even books. Two of the best are Jonathan Rosen's "The Ghost Bird," which appeared in the May 14, 2001, *New Yorker* magazine, and in Scott Weidensaul's book *The Ghost with Trembling Wings* (New York: North Point Press, 2002).

Dr. James Van Remsen, the man who organized the six-person search for the Ivory-bill, allowed me to interview him several times during the height of the media frenzy, including once in his office in Baton Rouge (see quotes, p. 151, "He passed with flying colors," and p. 155, "What about the *mites* . . . ?"). Cornell University Lab of Ornithology maintained updated information throughout the search on its superb Web site, www.birds.cornell.edu. The search team's conclusions were reported in "The 30-day Zeiss search for the ivory-billed woodpecker ends," Carl Zeiss Sports Optics news release, February 20, 2002.

Epilogue. Hope, Hard Work, and a Crow Named Betty

Everyone should read or reread Rachel Carson's *Silent Spring* (New York: Ballantine Books, 1962). It's beautifully written and as timely now as it ever was.

A great source of information about the Piping Plover and the Peregrine Falcon is the Web site of NatureServe, the organization that keeps track of species in trouble better than any I know. The Web site is easy to use. Just dial it up at www.natureserve.org and name your species. It offers good, detailed accounts of how a given species slipped into danger, where it continues to live, a history of efforts to help it, and what's being done for it now.

A fine book about animals that became extinct is Tim Flannery and Peter Schouten, *A Gap in Nature: Discovering the World's Extinct Animals* (New York: Atlantic Monthly Press, 2001).

Betty the Crow's breakthrough was a media sensation. The story "Crow Makes Wire Hook to Get Food," dated August 8, 2002, can be found on the National Geographic Web site. It even has, at this writing, moving pictures of Betty. The address is www.Nationalgeo graphic.com/news/2002/08/0808_020808_crow.html. For a magazine article, read "Shaping of Hooks in New Caledonian Crows," in *Science*, vol. 297, no. 5583, p. 981.

ACKNOWLEDGMENTS

If ever a book were like an ecosystem, this is it. I depended on the help of an interconnected web of scientists, conservationists, librarians, editors, guides, curators, translators, readers, and ordinary folks who often lived through extraordinary events.

For helping me comb through a mountain of material at Cornell University, I thank Susan Szasz Palmer and Elaine Engst of the Rare and Manuscript Collections Division. Likewise, Greg Budney and Marie Eckert at Cornell's Laboratory of Ornithology, Library of Natural Sounds, gave me much help and advice, and David C. Allen generously shared insights about his father, Arthur A. Allen.

For help in Madison Parish, Louisiana, I thank the Nature Conservancy's Keith Ouchley and Ronnie Ulmer—who gave up two days of his valuable time to guide me. Thanks also to Geneva Williams, Jerome Ford, Ava Kahn, and Tolbert Williams and the Madison Parish courthouse staff. Mary Tebo shared her valuable insights on the clearing of the southern forests. Tony Howe taught me about railroads.

For material and insights about German prisoners of war in Louisiana, I thank John Cherbini, Mary Sims, and Matthew Schott.

For sharing childhood memories of their lives in and around the Singer Tract, I thank Robert Fought, Gene and Lynelle Laird, and especially Billy Louis Fought, who helped me constantly and repeatedly.

I thank my Nature Conservancy colleagues Tony Grundhauser, Dean Harrison, John Humke, Becky Abel, Mike Andrews, and Will Stolzenberg, and especially Pat Patterson.

I visited Cuba to research this book. There I covered much ground, conducted many interviews, and made lifelong friends. I'm deeply grateful to Arturo Kirkconnell, Carlos Peña, Xiomara Gálvez Aguilera, Nils Navarro, Michael Sánchez, Ernesto Reyes, and Eduardo Fidalgo Franco. I thank Elizabeth García Guerra for helping me find the stamp of the Cuban Ivory-bill. I thank Dr. Lester Short for sharing memories of his visits to Cuba and insights about woodpeckers. I must also express my appreciation to Maine Congressman Tom Allen and his indomitable staffer Mark Oulette for helping me obtain a license to travel to Cuba. I thank Giraldo Alayón, Aimé Posada, and Mariela Machado González for friendship, insight, and inspiration.

I thank Longfellow Books, the world's greatest independent bookstore, especially Chris Bowe and Kirsten Cappy, for constant encouragement and uncritical love. The same goes for the Maine Writers and Publishers Alliance. For library research help, I thank Paul D'Alessandro of the Portland, Maine, Public Library, and Cassandra Fitzherbert and her fine staff at the University of Southern Maine's Interlibrary Loan Department.

I'm very grateful to Gavin Bauer and Tessa Hartley, both middle school students, who read this manuscript from front to back and gave me precise, constructive criticism. Thanks to Shoshana Hoose for reading and commenting on early drafts.

I can't thank my *amigo y compañero* Charles Duncan enough for going with me to Cuba, for translating, for taking photos, for helping me in so many ways. Likewise I thank the original Bromista, Ben Gregg, whose friendship means the world to me.

Many scientists, including Dr. Davis Finch and Dr. David Wilcove, helped me evaluate facts and ideas and led me to materials concerning everything from grubs to extinction. Dr. Larry Master, Chief Zoologist for NatureServe, read much of the scientific material critically and saved me from embarrassing errors. Dr. James Van Remsen, Curator of Birds at the LSU Museum of Natural Science, actually encouraged me to bombard him with a year's worth of questions. I thank him so much. Dr. Daniel Simberloff of the University of Tennessee's Department of Ecology and Evolutionary Biology read, admonished, encouraged, guided and mentored me through a great deal of this project, even when the Lady Vols experienced shaky times. I admire and thank him more than I can ever tell him. I thank Dr. Robert E. Jenkins for inspiring this book by expressing faith in me long ago and putting me to work in service of biodiversity. He is a genius and a kind man.

I am deeply indebted to my brilliant, caring editor Melanie Kroupa for taking on this project with me and guiding me through it. I could not have a better teammate. Thanks also to her assistant Sharon McBride, to the keen-eyed copy editors, Elaine Chubb and Susan Goldfarb, and to Barbara Grzeslo for her elegant design.

I could not have written this book without the support of my family. As it was written,

Hannah Hoose flew off to college and Ruby Hoose entered middle school. I thank them both so much for being such splendid daughters and wonderful people.

Above all, I thank Nancy Tanner. I had no idea what to expect when I contacted James Tanner's widow. Would she talk to me? What would she think about this project? She became a partner, corresponding with me through countless e-mails, letting me visit her, combing through files and sending photos, articles, and letters, coming up with ideas, nudging me away from wrong paths, even giving me advice on proper technique for the crawl stroke. Now I realize this book would not have been remotely possible without her. And I ended up with a fine friend into the bargain.

Finally, I thank *Campephilus principalis*, who lives, as Giraldo Alayón put it, between magic and science. I am lucky to have shared the earth for at least part of my life with such a magnificent creature as the Ivory-billed Woodpecker.

To learn about birds, ornithologists often
find themselves in precarious situations.
Here Jim Tanner tries to keep his balance
as he inspects a Bald Eagle nest on
Merritt Island, Florida, in 1935

PICTURE CREDITS

Courtesy of Xiomara Gálvez Aguilera, 15

Courtesy of Giraldo Alayón, v

Courtesy of the American Antiquarian Society, 39, 102

Courtesy of the American Philosophical Society, 9

The Charleston Museum, Charleston, South Carolina, 37

Department of Rare Books and Special Collections, University of Rochester Library, 41

Division of Rare and Manuscript Collections, Cornell University Library, 57, 63, 88, 179 (top), 185

Susan Roney Drennan—NAS, 44, 46, 51, 176 (top)

Ernst Mayr Library of the Museum of Comparative Zoology, Harvard University, 11, 34, 38, 171, 175

Courtesy of the Forest History Society, Durham, N.C., 28, 174

K. Fristrup, CLO, 146, 183

Hermione Museum, Tallulah, Louisiana, 117 (bottom), 124, 181

© Steven Holt/stockpix.com, 48

Phillip Hoose, 19, 136, 155

Ava Kahn/USFWS, 150

Courtesy of Gene Laird, 132

Collection of the Lauren Rogers Museum of Art Library, Laurel, Mississippi, 32, 117 (top)

Mark McRae, 12, 45, 173 (top)

National Archives, 128

National Audubon Society, 50

National Audubon Society, courtesy of Susan Roney Drennan, 27

Collection of The New-York Historical Society, 20, 22, 173 (bottom)

Courtesy of Carlos Peña, 134, 142, 145, 182

Courtesy of Perry Newspapers, Inc., Perry, Florida, 114, 180

Roger Tory Peterson Institute/ Seymour Levin photographer, 53

Courtesy of Nancy B. Tanner, v, 58, 61, 176 (bottom)

James T. Tanner, 68, 71, 74, 78, 80, 81, 82, 86, 87, 93, 96, 100, 103, 108 (both), 109, 111, 120, 148, 149, 165, 168, 177 (both), 179 (bottom), 188, endpapers

© Doug Wechsler/VIREO, 158, 184

INDEX

Page references in italics refer to illustrations.

192 *Index*